# Music Lessons

## Life Discovering Love, Truth, and Purpose

*Everett Daniel Cantagallo*

Music Lessons:
Life Discovering Love, Truth, and Purpose
Copyright © 2025 Everett Daniel Cantagallo

Produced and printed by Stillwater River Publications. All rights reserved. Written and produced in the United States of America. This book may not be reproduced or sold in any form without the expressed, written permission of the author(s) and publisher.

Visit our website at
*www.StillwaterPress.com*
for more information.

First Stillwater River Publications Edition.

ISBN: 978-1-968548-14-8

1 2 3 4 5 6 7 8 9 10

Written by Everett Daniel Cantagallo.
Cover & interior book design by Matthew St. Jean.
Published by Stillwater River Publications,
West Warwick, RI, USA.

*The views and opinions expressed in this book are solely those of the author(s) and do not necessarily reflect the views and opinions of the publisher.*

*I dedicate this book to my youngest grandson,
Maxwell Joseph Cantagallo. It was his interest in
my life and writing that gave me motivation to
complete this project. Thanks Max.*

## Preface

Fresh air, movement of my body, lungs, and heart, give me a restorative feeling. My best ideas come to me when exercising outdoors, be it a refreshing walk, scenic bike ride, leisurely swim or kayaking rhythmically on a pond; even undertaking manual labor outdoors, allows me to contemplate higher thoughts. Each performance helps clear my head, allowing me time to think of life's purpose. I entertain myself with endless possibilities of life. My mind can be a pleasant place to spend time, but with imagination, my thoughts can become whimsical or exaggeratedly idealistic. One of the ways to tame this stream of thought and imagination is to write. My desk is full of half-finished projects and undeveloped ideas. It is the writing process that is therapeutic, enjoyable, and for me, sloppy. I write on any paper scraps, pads, or notebooks available, transfer the promising ideas to an outline and research the material. Through writing I relearn what I've forgotten. I write what interests me, and what I believe, finding a connection between the two, I organize the bits and pieces of paper and constantly rewrite. My goal in writing this narrative is to leave a legacy to my children and grandchildren, but more than that, to leave behind a positive message of hope and encouragement. This impetus was strong allowing me to embody my beliefs in a small easy to read paperback.

In John Bunyan's Christian allegory "The Pilgrim's Progress" the main character, Christian, has a journey filled with trials and tribulations. Christian encounters people and signs along his path to Heaven's gate, the signs are both helpful and deceiving. The Holy Word and pop music are two guides along my life's pilgrimage. Pop music for me can be both entertaining and beneficial. The Spirit of Truth works in my consciousness at the intersection of reason and faith allowing me to find connections to the tangible and spiritual aspects of life. Certain popular music melodies and lyrics validate my belief. Mindfulness helps me see truth and meaning in everyday life, including listening to music. I find a connection to others and reassurance of my purpose with simple pursuits of daily living.

The first twenty-eight years of my life were spent in Providence, RI. The word providence means, "The protective care of God." In 1636 Roger Williams an English Theologian, named the area in honor of "God's merciful providence." Born, raised, educated, married, started a family, and began a career all within Providence city's limits. I was brought up by an enthusiastic Italian Catholic mother, I attended parochial schools; except for one year, a Catholic grammar school, high school, and college. My education took place within a two-mile radius of where I grew up. I learned to reason in a tiny section of planet earth on a path that became defined only as I looked back. "Life can only be understood backwards, but it must be lived forwards." Soren Kierkegaard

My teachers in Catholic education had Mission Statements. In elementary school my teachers were the School Sisters of Notre Dame. Their Mission Statement: **"Our mission is to proclaim the good news as School Sisters of Notre Dame, directing our entire lives toward that oneness for which Jesus Christ was sent. As he was sent to show the Father's love to the world, we are sent to make Christ visible by our very being, by sharing our love, faith, and hope."**

In high school, the teaching Christian Brothers of LaSalle Academy's Mission: **"Guided by faith, service, and community our brothers are part of something truly special, a global network of teachers and scholars, united by centuries old Roman Catholic mission to serve others through education that embraces all."**

Providence College is a Catholic university

founded by the Dominican Order also called the order of preachers. Mission Statement: **"To proclaim the word of God by preaching, teaching, and example. To bring the message of Jesus Christ, mercy, and compassion to people in and out of season. Their life in common along with study and prayer, allows them to share the fruits of contemplation and proclaim the good news to every land and nation." The Dominican order's mottos, In Latin "Laudare, Benedicere, Praedicare." To praise, to bless, to teach. "Veritas" Truth and "Contemplare et Contemplata aliis Tradere" to contemplate and give to others the fruit of contemplation.**

These are the true teachings of my education in Providence, Rhode Island. This is my foundation of a life built on faith and reason. These institutions taught me how to think of God, Jesus, and the Holy Spirit while living in the secular world. This is my life living with the power of the word, not always a straight road, however, a path guided by good counsel.

In my career in business, I worked for and represented companies that had solid mission statements. The best companies never lost sight of their mission. Those were the companies people wanted to work for, those were the companies that flourished. The culture of these companies was to serve and in serving others they in turn attained their goals. My gratitude is to the teachers who followed and lived up to their missions. Thank you for sharing your faith through example as well as teaching. A companion to my formal education was listening to the radio and popular music of my time. The composers and lyricist who stayed true to their music thrived and produced beautiful sounds, sharing their insights of love with the listeners. "Without music, life would be a mistake." Friedrich Nietzsche

CHAPTER ONE

## A Sentimental Journey

"Of all the pursuits open to men, the search for wisdom is most perfect, more sublime, more profitable, and more full of joy."

THOMAS AQUINAS
*Theologian, Philosopher, Dominican preacher,*
*Angelic Doctor (1225–1274)*

The beginnings of my relationship with music took place in a cellar of an apartment house. My earliest recollection of hearing an amazing sound was when I was four years old. My younger brother and I sat silently in the basement of my grandfather's apartment house where he often practiced playing his trumpet. The basement was cave-like with a stone foundation and gravel floor. The space was dry, dusty, and daunting to my brother and me. Grandpa Johny was a band leader, and a trumpet player. My mother had dropped us off for a special appointment, a doctor's visit and time spent alone with my grandmother. Mom was in a bind because our grandpa John rarely babysat us. Grandfather was an imposing figure; he stood over six feet tall with jet black hair and a thin pencil mustache. In later years, his appearance reminded me of the Medici family from the Renaissance Florence. He had that look and Tuscan demeanor; we obeyed every directive he gave, "You boys sit here and don't make a peep." We had walked down a wide bending wooden staircase which opened to a large center room with a huge white asbestos covered furnace. A dirty Persian rug lay in front of the furnace. Under a bright light bulb hanging by a long cord from a wooden rafter, a music rack holding grandpa's sheet music stood. It looked like a lone sentinel guarding a massive white castle. Over to our right was a dark wooden coal bin with a wood chute extending down from the cellar window. In a small room to the left behind a green opened planked door was my young uncle John Boy's elaborate miniature train set. John Boy was our favorite playmate at the apartment house. I remember him inviting us in and running his Lionel trains for our enjoyment. The train set, built on a raised platform, bellowed smoke as it passed tiny towns, crossed metal bridges, and disappeared under mountains made of paper mâché. The old coal bin and the train room were places that ignited my imagination, what fun my brother and I could have had if we were only able to move off our seats. Grandpa started to blow into his trumpet starting with the music scale. He played the same notes over and over. It was boring. Once he had warmed up an incredibly different sound filled the dusty air. He looked down at the sheet music and started to put those notes together. It was the first time I heard live music. The music moved me. Sitting quietly was no longer a restriction as my ears were set free. The way the trumpet moved in my grandfather's hand was mesmerizing. It was like I was deaf and now I could hear. My brother and I had a front row seat to a private performance. The first song my grandfather played was, "Sentimental Journey" by Doris Day – written by John T Williams, Bud Green, and Benjamin Homer.

Nineteen years passed and as a wedding present my grandfather paid for his band to play at our reception and Sentimental Journey was the last number he played. It was also the last song I ever saw my grandfather perform. He was quite the entertainer; my new bride and I sat quietly and did not make a peep while listening to this enchanting song sending us off on our marital journey.

When I was eleven years old, I joined the boy scouts. Our troop leader was also a musician, he knew my grandfather. The troop needed a bugler and because my grandfather was a well-known trumpet player, our troop leader thought I was the perfect candidate. I never played a musical instrument of any type and had no desire. Reluctantly accepting the position, I took the bugle home and learned to play two songs by ear, reveille, and taps. Being an adaptive learner by the next scout meeting I was able to play taps at the end of our monthly get-together. Luckily, that was sufficient. I remember blowing into couch cushions to muffle the sound, sparing my family and the tenants in the above apartments the pain of listening to my learning curve. I did not have a love for playing the horn like my grandfather but made the commitment as a resolute boy scout, trustworthy, loyal, clean, brave, and reverent. Unlike my grandpa, I did not play notes, rather I played sounds. Time passed and my enjoyment of listing to good music never waned. "A song is the exultation of the mind dwelling on eternal things, bursting forth in the voice." Thomas Aquinas

Listening to music releases the neurotransmitter dopamine in the brain. Dopamine sends pleasure signals to the rest of the body and along with an increase in the levels of serotonin, the mood in the listener changes and the mind is calm, free from anxiety. I like that feeling and still do appreciate it every time I listen to my favorite songs. "True music must repeat the thought and inspiration of the people and the time." George Gershwin (1898-1937) American composer.

The soundtrack of my life is a story of those feelings. feelings of emotions, pleasurable thoughts, and relationships. My imaginational response to music is an emotional river, and my Catholic Christian education an anchor in that river, not allowing me to float too far down stream. Artists that appeal to my senses, write, and sing of deep thoughts and experiences. The pop songs that attract me, tell a story, give advice, inform, and make me feel like I belong, same as Christianity. Pop music gives me a sense of connection with people and a much stronger connection with universal feelings. The songs I relate to have good Lyrics, great melodies, harmonies, rhythm, wonderful voices, and meanings that touch my soul. I enjoy low-key ballads, like love songs. Love songs express a deep emotion. A sensation in the soul, mind, and body. This reaction is recognized by the listeners, but where does it originate? This common knowledge of an influence that is good and pure must have come from somewhere; it is an understanding of the heart as opposed to the mind. "At the center of your being you have the answer; you know who you are, and you know what you want." Lao Tzu, Ancient Chinese Philosopher (6 BC-5 BC). "One word frees us of all the weight and pain in life, that word is Love." Sophocles an ancient Greek Playwright (496BC-406BC). In the Christian gospel of John 13: 34-35 (WEB) Jesus tells his disciples to Love one another. *"A new commandment I give to you, that you love one another. Just as I have Loved you, you also love one another. By this everyone will know that you are my disciples, if you have love for one another."* Matthew 22:37-40 (WEB) *"Jesus said to him, 'you shall love the Lord your God with all your heart, with all your soul, and with all your mind.' This is the first and great commandment. A second likewise is this, 'you shall love your neighbor as yourself.' The whole law and the prophets depend on these two commandments."* There is also a huge benefit in loving, as told by the apostle Peter in the New Testament. 1 Peter 4:7-8 (WEB) *"But the end of all things is near. Therefore be of sound mind, self-controlled, and sober in prayer. And above all things be earnest in your love among yourselves, for love covers a multitude of sins."*

So how does this relate to the Spirit of Truth, Love, and Music Lessons?

In the beginning of my pop musical journey the Beach Boys and specifically Brian Wilson's lyrics spoke to me through his music. Spending hours listening to Beach Boy albums on my cousin's new stereo record player, time effortlessly flew by. Lost in thought listening, I learned to think beyond the sounds of the music. I started to hear a message delivered in the song. It was not only the songs of surfing, cars, and summer, it was Brian Wilson's delivering meaning in lyrics with "God only Knows," "Good Vibrations," "In my Room," The Warmth of the Sun," "surf's up," and "Don't worry Baby." Brian Wilson showed me his vulnerability; he delved deeper into his feelings. He showed me that insecurity was normal. I did not need to be unfeeling or alone. I could be OK without being a tough guy, as portrayed in the song, "I am a rock; I am an Island" by Simon and Garfunkel written by Paul Simon. Brian Wilson's songs were very relatable to what I was going through in my life. They still are today when I listen to his recent music, songs like "Love and Mercy," Your Imagination" "This Beautiful Day," "Tell me why," "Our Special Love," and "The right time." In a close second place, the Beatles also had an influence on my exploration of life and love. The Lennon-McCartney team could paint a beautiful picture in my young mind of relationships and emotions. George Harrison proved to be a good influence with his lyrics and insightful song writing. I have read that surrounded by his family and friends, George Harrison, who died on November 29, 2001, often said "Everything can wait but the search for God cannot wait and love one another."

Music and lyrics helped me learn about the power of love and its connection to living a fuller life. It is in the way artists write and express love that I feel a relationship between the music and my faith. My mind and heart hear and relate to a message in a song. I hear a voice of reason and a spirit of truth in the music. In listening to the human expressions of love I am mindful of God and the people I have loved, and question if it was deep enough. Did I give all I could, and can I give more? The feelings in the music I enjoy resonate Christian and Judeo teachings, to love one another and treat others as I wish to be treated. The artist's personal attitudes of life may or may not be like mine, however the message perceived from popular love songs strengthen my belief in the invisible power of love and its source.

CHAPTER TWO

## Back Where You Belong

We are living in a time of a constant flow of information, so much truth overwhelms, and the words collide with each other leaving questions on which truth is the most important. Common sense does not prevail in the dialogue. What flag do I want to fly? What colors do I dare show? It is during these moments that I find comfort in the music of my youth and the lessons they deliver. I return to my core Christian belief. This experience is not unique to any generation; it is part of a personal pilgrimage. A journey of seeking answers to our existence, the why and purpose of life; along with Faith, Hope, and Love, one of my vehicles of seeking answers is pop music. I also find comfort and support in theology, philosophy, literature, poetry, theater, and the other arts, I recognize the influences of them all within a popular song.

In ancient times great thinkers and moral teachers gathered people around in small groups, and exchanged ideas with them, sharing thoughts and truths on different subjects. The great philosophers and enlightened sages of antiquity such as Socrates, Plato, and Aristotle have influenced thought for 26 centuries. They showed us that by observing and questioning life we can discover the existence of the human soul, virtues, moral truth, and beauty. The ancient teachers gave us the first University of the western world; and in the pursuit of wisdom, they challenge us today to think of an ideal society with Justice, Beauty, and Equality. Lamenting the current world events, a friend once asked where I thought the solution could be found. I did not hesitate, the only true solution is found within us in Faith, Hope and Love. "The unexamined life is not worth living." Socrates- Ancient Greek Philosopher (470 BC-399 BC). "False words are not only evil in themselves, but they infect the soul with evil." Plato- Ancient Greek Philosopher-student of Socrates (429 BC – 347 BC). "There is only one way to avoid criticism: do nothing, say nothing, and be nothing." Aristotle – Ancient Greek Philosopher- student of Plato (384 BC-322 BC).

These great thinkers also recognized the relationship between music and emotions. Philosophers discussed music as a warning as well as a benefit to human life. "Music is a moral law. It gives soul to the universe, wings to the mind, flight to the imagination, and charm and gaiety to life and to everything." Plato, Greek Philosopher (429 BC – 347 BC).

Working on our bucket list my wife and dear friends visited the ruins of antiquity, Rome, Greece, and Ephesus in Türkiye. There in the plaza of the ancient library of Celsus, in Ephesus, on a stone pedestal, Saint Paul the Apostle (10 AD-67AD) would preach the good news to anyone who would listen. I was happy to be standing in that place of biblical significance and closing my eyes imagined what it felt like to hear Paul's message in person. At the time of Paul's ministry, the population of Ephesus was approximately 250,000. Paul's Listening audience was small in comparison but always moving with new curious minds. Greeks, Romans, slaves, and freemen from the Roman Empire, walked by interested in fresh ideas on life's purpose. Paul delivered a new message of hope and love, a message of the resurrected son of God, a redeemer for humanity. *"that he would grant you, according the riches of his glory, that you may to be strengthened with power through his Spirit in the person, that Christ may dwell in your hearts through faith, to the end that you being rooted and grounded in love, may be strengthened to comprehend with all the saints what is the width and length and height and depth, and to know Christ's love which surpasses knowledge, so that you may be filled with all the fullness of God"* EPHESIANS 3:16-19 (WEB)

Today the chatter and volume of ideas and opinions are emotionally explosive. Overwhelmed with information, I am sometimes conflicted. Common sense is not too common. Yet with all this news and distraction, I can still feel the invisible wave of love. "God is unchanging in his Love. He loves you. He has a plan for your life. Don't let the newspaper headlines frighten you. God is still sovereign; He's still on the throne." Billy Graham- William Franklin Graham Jr. (1918-2018) American Evangelist, Southern Baptist minister, and civil rights advocate. In Music Lessons, I want to show how this wave of love uses pop music to support my ideas of life, marriage, family, and community. More importantly music helps me to Learn how It all leads to one place for those who seek. The bible tells us to look at life and learn by using our senses. The ancient philosophers knew how powerful observation and contemplation persist. This is not a new concept, existing since the beginning of recorded time, Jesus Christ teaches the concept in relation to God, himself, and the Holy Spirit. I have often thought how easy it should have been for the people who had seen and listened to Jesus to believe in him. It was not easy even after they experienced all he had to offer; it was as though they did not want to acknowledge his truth and beauty. It has been true since the fall of man and is still true today, that for selfish reasons humans reject the truth and want to be the truth themselves. *"Having eyes, don't you see? Having ears, don't you hear? Don't you remember?"* Mark 8:18 (WEB) *"In them the prophecy of Isaiah is fulfilled, which says, by hearing you will hear, and in no way understand; Seeing you will see, and will in no way perceive, for this people's heart has grown callous, their ears are dull of hearing, and they have closed their eyes, or else perhaps they might perceive with their eyes, hear with their ears, understand with their heart, and would turn again, and I would heal them."* Matthew 13:14-15 (WEB) *"Ask and it will be given you, Seek, and you will find. Knock and it will be opened for you."* Matthew 7:7 (WEB)

CHAPTER THREE

## Sweet Lord

*L**ove* is the spirit of life; it is the fruit of the Holy Spirit. The Holy Spirit or Spirit of God means breath or wind in the languages of the bible. Who can live without breath? Throughout the centuries believers have given it various names; the Spirit of God, the Spirit of Truth, the Holy Ghost, and the Holy Spirit of promise. The Holy Spirit is a person of the Trinity of God. An explanation that opened my mind concerning the Holy Spirt is one I heard from C.S. Lewis (1898-1963) the famous teacher, writer, philosopher, and theologian. My gramma schoolteachers taught me there are three persons in one God, The Father (Yahweh), his Son (Jesus Christ) and his spirit The Holy Ghost or The Holy Spirit. The best reasoning that my Catholic nun and teacher had to offer was it is a mystery, we are to take it on faith. I had no problem with that answer and for a long time I viewed Jesus as the son of God, just like I was the son of my father, and after Jesus's death, Jesus sent the Holy Spirit down to earth to continue his work. It was not until reading and listening to C.S. Lewis that it all became clearer. In the book "Mere Christianity" C.S. Lewis explains the Trinity in this manner; God begot his son; God and his son begot the Holy Spirit through love and all three are present in the creation of everything. Lewis makes a distinction between begetting and creating, when an entity is begotten, it is brought forth in a manner like its source. It implies a continuity of nature. A lion begets cubs, and they inherit the nature of lions. Humans beget offsprings who in turn inherit the nature of humans. When a thing is created it involves making that which is different than the creator. A lion makes a den for her cubs. A human paints pictures or makes a sculpture. These are inanimate objects or creations with no consciousness or spirit. So, when we say that God begets Jesus, we mean Christ has the same nature as God. When I look at Jesus Christ in this way it brings me to a better understanding of the Gospels of Matthew, Mark, Luke, and John. It becomes clearer on how the human Jesus could do and say all that he did. It was in his nature to do so, as Luke tells the story of Jesus at twelve years old who had no formal education or teachings in the Jewish Law. Luke 2:46-47 (WEB) ***"It happened after three days they found him in the temple, sitting in the midst of the teachers, both listening to them, and asking them questions. All who*** *heard him were amazed at his understanding and his answers."* The same with the Holy Spirit, we affirm that both Jesus and the Holy Ghost are fully God and not merely creations of God. They are eternal and have equality with God the Father possessing the same nature. The Holy Spirit is a person, we use the word person only as a means of understanding in a human manner, the third entity of the Trinity and an inconceivable Power. Genesis 1: 1-2 (WEB) *"In the beginning God created the heavens and the earth. Now the earth was formless and empty. Darkness was on the surface of the deep. God's Spirit was hovering over the surface of the waters."*

John 14:16-17 (WEB) *"I will pray to the Father, and he will give you another Counselor, that he may be with you forever the Spirit of truth, whom the world can't receive, for it doesn't see him and doesn't know him. You know him, for he lives with you and will be in you."* John 14:26 (WEB) *"But the Counselor, the Holy Spirit, whom the Father will send in my name, will teach you all things, and will remind you of all that I said to you,"* Acts 1:8 (WEB) *"But you will receive power when the holy Spirit has come upon you. You will be witnesses to me in Jerusalem, in all Judea and Samaria, and to the uttermost parts of the earth."* Romans 8:26 (WEB) *"In the same way, the Spirit also helps our weakness; for we do not know how to pray as we ought. But the Spirit himself makes intercession for us with groanings which can't be uttered."* 1Corinthians 12:7 (WEB) *"But to each one is given the manifestation of the Spirit for the profit of all."* Galatians 5: 22-23 (WEB) *"But the fruit of the Spirit is love, joy, peace, patience, kindness, goodness, faithfulness, gentleness, and self-control. Against such things there is no law."* "Every truth without exception-and whoever may utter it-is from the Holy Spirit." Thomas Aquinas. Luke 11:13 (WEB) *"If you then, being evil, know how to give good gifts to your children, how much more will your heavenly Father in heaven give the Holy Spirit to those who ask him?"*

CHAPTER FOUR

## The Beat Goes On

Welcome to my Music Lessons. Music Lessons will not be complete without reading the lyrics, listening to the songs, and connecting scriptures to the messages sung. The message of a song is heightened by the emotion that a song delivers to your heart and mind. I urge you to stop reading and listen to the songs in each chapter to get a better understanding of the synergies expressed. I wanted to show key lyrics on all the songs that I mention, however that would be an infringement on copyrights. All these lyrics and songs appear online. Enjoy listening with the Spirit of God in mind. Sometime, the lesson in a song may only be a phrase which awakens a deep spiritual feeling, while at other times the message will be clearer and straight forward. The singer may know or not understand the message but will deliver it with all their talent in the style of the times. The music composer and lyricist will know exactly how the message fits in the composition, while musicians will keep the rhythm, the beat, and sound moving into our mind, body, and soul.

Music Lessons are signs along my highway of life. Signs that make me question circumstances surprise me with insights, make me think of time eternal and love. An example of what I mean by a Music Lesson is the song **"You've got a friend"** by **Carole King**. The lyricist and singer, Carole King composes a beautiful song of friendship and what the Greeks call PHILIA, a love shown within close friendship. When I hear the message of this song, one of a friend to call on in times of trouble and doubt, I relate it to God's love for his creations. Whenever I am fearful or troubled, I pray for clarity and someone greater than myself to light my way. "We set forth our petitions before God, not in order to make known to him our needs and desires, but rather so that we ourselves may realize that in these things it is necessary to turn to God for help." Thomas Aquinas.

The Holy Spirit teaches and reminds. This song "You've got a friend" reminds me of Psalm 34 from the Old Testament. Psalm 34: 17-18 (WEB) ***"The righteous cry, and the LORD hears, and delivers them out of all their troubles. The LORD is near to those who have a broken heart; and saves those who have a crushed spirit."*** The Holy Spirit confirms our relationship with God; hearing this song strikes a chord in my heart, God hears our cry for help, and I have a personal relationship with his Spirit. This message helps me deal with my individual experiences and emotional pain. The Lesson also makes me think about my faith and where I can go in my darkest hour to find comfort. A song with a similar theme is Motown's hit "Reach Out (I'll Be There)" by The Four Tops, written by Holland-Dozier-Holland and Collins. Reach out for God. It may not be what the writers intended. It is truth when I view it in terms of my belief. I also enjoy listening to these songs. They unwind me and calm my mind allowing a few minutes to meditate on a message of comfort and Hope and a reminder of a well-worn path to Love.

All loves eventually leads to that ultimate love which the Greeks call AGAPE, the unconditional love of our Father and the Spirit shown to us through his son Jesus Christ, whose love is King. This next song gives an emotional boost to my thought of God's Love. Sade's song "Your love is King" written by **Sade Adu** and **Stuart Matthewman. I** realize it is a love song written for two human beings, but its beauty transcends human love. To me God's Love is king. I am thankful and grateful for the love given unconditionally. I am not worthy of this type of love. I have done nothing to merit the gift. In fact, I have done things to be undeserving of it. This love is sometimes called amazing Grace. "Amazing Grace" by Celtic Woman written by John Newton English Anglican Clergyman and poet (1725-1807). "Amazing grace how sweet the sound, I once was lost but now am found."

Here is a thought from a Priest, poet, writer and a liberation theologian from Nicaragua, Ernesto Cardenal. In 1974, my mother was dying of cancer and a friend of hers sent her a book called "To live is to love" by Ernesto Cardenal. I found and read the book after her death and through the years his words shine bright in my mind. I looked up and read his biography recently. He died on my birthday March 1st in 2020. "We turn outward, attracted by the beauty we see in created things without realizing that they are only a reflection of real beauty. And the real beauty is within us." Ernesto Cardenal (1925-2020). Real beauty is within us as is truth and real love, sometimes it needs a jolt for us to remember and for me that jolt comes in the form of a good love song. "Most persons are so absorbed in the contemplation of the outside world that they are wholly oblivious to what is passing on within themselves." Nikola Tesla (1856-1943) Serbian – American inventor.

Since 1964, music, specifically in the top forty radio format, has been a favorite teacher. Listening to pop music, from a discarded, broken, tan colored, RCA tube radio, found in a junk pile of a local privately owned city gas station, I developed a persona. The melodies and lyrics created a place of refuge from a tumult life, for me music opened a wide variety of life's experiences. Music allowed me to dream and fabricate in my mind a sanctuary from roles forced upon me and roles I took on. Imagination turned into reality and color replaced a black and white existence. "Life isn't about finding yourself. Life is about creating yourself. Better keep yourself clean and bright you are the window through which you must see the world." George Bernard Shaw (1856-1950) playwright, critic, and Political activist. This was good advice at the time, yet I was too young to realize that I was not the designer nor the creator of my life. "Our greatest ability as humans is not to change the world, but to change ourselves." Mahatma Gandhi (1869-1948), Indian Lawyer, non-violent activist.

Religious studies, history, philosophy, poetry, and literature from attending Catholic schools along with the tunes of the time, abled me to patch together a guidebook for living. The music of my mentors, top forty pop radio songs, along with a Catholic education, anchored me. My foundation was solid and during the storms of the later years, I had a rock to rebuild upon. I cannot name every song in my education, as I cannot narrate every spiritual lesson, so I will limit myself in each phase of my Music lessons.

A news article appeared online. It was an

announcement of singer Tony Bennett's struggle with Alzheimer's disease. Tony has passed away. The article said that Tony had continued to sing and play music at home to help stimulate his brain in positive ways. I read a while ago that music stimulates the two hemispheres of our brains. This is quite a simple explanation of how music affects the body. Today science is making great strides in helping people, especially older adults manage pain, depression and dementia using music therapy. Modern day brain imaging dives much deeper in discovering the total brain's reaction to listening to music. Music has life-enhancing abilities. "What the mind believes the body achieves," is a saying used by athletes; however it can be applied to life and living. Music helps the mind to believe in life again and stir up emotions that have laid dormant for various reasons.

Music, especially pop music, has been a constant companion for a long time. Once on a business trip, I was in Downtown Cleveland. Cleveland is the home of the Rock and Roll Hall of Fame. I was not going to waste my opportunity of being so close to the Rock and Roll Hall without a visit. I took the next day off from work and walked from my hotel along a World War One memorial stairway down to the venue, the walk itself was emotionally stirring. I have always been interested in the events of the Great War. Recalling my teachings, readings, and movies on World War

One made the walk stimulating and enjoyable. The day at the hall flew by. It was like visiting a religious shrine, full of prophets, poets, sinners, and saints. While walking along the path of rock and roll history, I remembered lyrics from Alannah Myles song "Black Velvet" by Canadian songwriters Christopher Ward and David Tyson. This song is a tribute to the beginning of rock and roll and Elvis Presley. There is a verse that talks of rock and roll as a new religion. That verse is not too far from the constructive interaction I am talking about. I relate my visit to the Rock and Roll Hall and the emotions it stirred to walking down the streets of ancient Rome and visiting the many Catholic Basilicas and admiring the unbelievable artistic works of Michelangelo, Maderno, Bernini, and other great artists. I am not elevating the works of singers and song writers to the great artists of the Renaissance; I am simply stating that our senses can produce emotions that lead to conscious thought of connections in our soul.

CHAPTER FIVE

## What Is It All About?

There is a point in everyone's life when the question arises, what is Important? The Holy Spirit teaches and reminds us of what is important in our fleeting time on earth. As time went by what I once thought was a worthwhile life, hard work, sacrifice, making money, and the pursuit of happiness, resulted in empty promises and chasing after the wind. True love is the only worthy quest. In love we become an earnest partner, have a good marriage, a loving home and family. We become the person we are meant to be. "No man truly has joy unless he lives in Love." Thomas Aquinas. The famous teacher, writer, philosopher and theologian, C.S. Lewis authored a book called "The Four Loves." In America we have one word for love. I love my wife, children, grandchildren, friends, neighbors, pets, cars, trucks, food, and other things. Do I love them all the same? I think not. The

Greek's had six words for love along with two more philosophical concepts of love. Four distinct words for love are in C.S. Lewis's books "Mere Christianity," and "The Four Loves." Their meanings are expressed in the Christian bibles and other faith's scripts. There are love songs in my pop music Lessons, along with biblical truths, that connect to each of the loves that C.S. Lewis describes in his recorded talks and writings. The four main words for Love are STORGE, PHILIA, EROS, and AGAPE.

One of my favorite Books of the Bible is The Book of TOBIT. The Book of Tobit is found in the Catholic, Eastern Orthodox Bibles, and the Dead Sea Scrolls. The story is included in Jewish teachings and can be read online in the World English Bible Catholic edition, (WEBC). It is a story of faith, the answer to prayer, an adventure story with an angel, demon and two young lovers. The author is unknown, and the story is a great mix of creativity and theological teachings. All four loves mentioned above can be found in this short story of a Jewish father and son living in captivity of the rulers of ancient Nineveh in the seventh century BC. Themes of love, forgiveness, righteousness, marriage, family, community, gratitude, and praise to God permeate the Book of TOBIT. The Book of Tobit is analogous to me as a good love song. Tobit 13:6 (WEBC) ***"IF you turn to him with your whole heart and with your whole soul, to do truth*** *before him, then he will turn to you, and won't hide his face from you. See what he will do with you. Give him thanks with your whole mouth bless the Lord of righteousness. Exalt the everlasting King. I give him thanks in the land of my captivity and show his strength and majesty to a nation of sinners. Turn, you sinners, and do righteousness before him. Who can tell if he will accept you and have mercy on you?"*

A pop music song that comes to mind when I read these verves is the song by Seals and Crofts, "Get Closer" written by Jim Seels and Dash Crofts. If we want God in our life then we must actively seek him, get closer to him and he in turn will get closer to us. James 4:8 (WEB) ***"Come near to God and he will come near to you."***

CHAPTER SIX

*It Is a Family Affair*

STORGE – This is a Greek word for familial Love, like that found between members of a family. The love a mother has for her children, the love a son has for his father, love between sisters, brothers, mothers, fathers, grandparents, aunts, uncles, and cousins. "It's not the love you make. It's the love you give." Nikola Tesla. 1 Timothy 5:8 (WEB) *"But if anyone doesn't provide for his own, and especially his own household, he has denied the faith and is worse than an unbeliever."* Acts 16:30-31 *"He then brought them out and asked, 'Sirs, what must I do to be saved?' They replied, 'Believe in the Lord Jesus, and you will be saved-you and your household."* Examples of this type of love (STORGE) in modern pop music that I enjoy are "We are Family" by Sister Sledge, written by Nile Rodgers and Bernard Edwards. This song is for the lucky eleven sisters in our family. "Mama" by

B.J. Thomas written by Mark Charron and "A song for mama" by Boyz II Men written by Babyface, songs with heartfelt lyrics for mom. "Teach your children well" by Crosby, Stills, Nash, and Young. Through our example our children will continue our legacy. "Shower the People" by James Taylor. We must never hide our Love for each other. Disagreements yes, forgiveness yes, hate no. "Let Your Love Flow" by the Bellamy brothers written by Larry E. Williams. In every season we let our love show within our family. "Leader of the Band" by Dan Fogelberg. This song is for my grandfather who was the leader of his band. "My father's eyes" by Eric Clapton. We remember the good in our parents and grandparents, their good helped us raise our children. "Dance with my father "by Luther Vandross written by Luther Vandross and Richard Marx. To be loved is the best feeling in the entire world. "Rock and roll lullaby" by BJ Thomas written by **Barry Mann and Cynthia Weil. We rock our babies and give them comfort, we sing to them, and they open a world of wonder and love unconditionally.** "Isn't she lovely" by Stevie Wonder. The beauty and innocence of a baby is unsurpassed. It softens a hard heart. "Father and Daughter" by Paul Simon. Our daughters think we are the best and that makes us a little better than we are. "Daughters" by John Mayer. May every parent live long enough to see the rose bloom in their daughter's life. "The Last

Song" by Elton John written by Elton John and Bernie Taupin. I do not care who you are or what you have done, as a parent I will not forsake you.

When I was young, my father would take me to visit my grandparents every Saturday. They lived on five acres of land a short ride from the city of Providence, RI. My grandfather immigrated to America from Ferrentino, Italy about forty miles outside Rome. He and my grandmother recreated life from that small commune in Italy. My grandparents' land was small but full of diversity. There were flower and vegetable gardens, fruit trees, grape vines, a goat tied under a mulberry tree, multiple sheds with chicken and rabbit coops built from any type of scrap materials available. My grandfather also ran an Italian American social club on the same property. A small red brick building built sometime in the 1920's, still standing to this day, served as a meeting place in the Italian American expatriate community. My favorite memories as a young boy revolve around working in the garden and social club during summer's school vacation. At five pm every summer night the first-generation of American Italian men would stop by for beers and fresh boiled sweet corn on the cob, picked fresh in season from the garden. The beers cost five cents a glass and the sweet corn with butter ten cents a cob. The young men were labors, building Rhode Island's emerging thoroughfare interstate route 95. Arriving dirty, tired, and thirsty, our Pisani did not stay long. As young family men they had a short window to get a cold beer, a quick snack, and be home on time for their family dinner. Grandpa and I would clean up after the rush. My job was to rag mop with bucket the muddy tile floor. After cleaning up, Grandpa and I went into the house for dinner. At night, the social club was a gathering place for older expatriates from Italy. On warm summer nights I ran pitchers of a locally brewed lager beer called Narragansett, from the social club out to a dimly lit patio. A large apple tree and a leafy grape vine covered a half paved and grass patio. Old Italian men sat around a thick oak table with huge animal paws on its pedestal. They sat on a mishmash of secondhand chairs with their feet on the worn grass. Playing cards under the apple tree, in the fruit, vegetable, and cigar scented summer air, they spoke mostly in their Romanesco dialect. To pay for drinks they played Morra. Morra is an Italian finger game. Like the odd and even finger game we played as kids on the streets of Providence. The men would stand up, face one another, count to three in Italian, (Uno, Due, Tre) and throw one hand with a random number of fingers extended and shout at the top of their lungs a number from one to ten in Italian. They would play until someone shouted the correct number of the fingers thrown. The loser paid for the pitcher of beer. This is how I learned to count to ten in Italian. Grandpa also had two bocce courts near the patio, along with a horseshoe lane. The neighborhood Italian immigrants drank beer, homemade wine, and smoked Italian stogie cigars. They spoke about life and the villages of their birth. With sentimental looks in their eyes; the old men talked of one day returning to the old country and the loved ones they left behind years ago. The first wave of Italian settlers never did return to Italy. Next to the patio was a shed with containers of seed from the former year's crops and an old coal stove the family used to cook and jar the tomatoes in late summer. The shed had no electricity only a homemade rickety door to keep out rain and snow. One warm late summer night as I was running from the club to the patio, I glanced over at my grandfather. He was happy drinking and talking with friends, but I noticed how frail and weak he looked. I suddenly realized that someday he was going to die. That moment of realization overwhelmed me. I loved him very much. After serving the drinks, I ran into that dark shed with the dirt floor and coal stove. Overwhelmed with sorrow, I started to cry. Grandpa followed me and asked what was wrong. I did not know what to say. What do you say? He hugged me and said, "Non essere disturbato" in his broken English "do not be troubled whatever it is will pass." I always get emotional thinking of those summer nights when I listen to songs like, "Memories" by Elvis Presley written by Billy Strange and Mac Davis, "Times of your life" by Paul Anka, "Try to Remember" by Josh Groban written by American lyricist Tom Jones and Harvey Schmidt, "Through the years" by Kenny Rogers written by Steve Dorff and Marty Panzer and my favorite "I wanna go back" by Eddie Money written by Monty Byrom, Danny Chauncey, and Ira Walker. Songs like these bring heart and mind to the people I love who are no longer with us. I could go on for a long time with this type of song. There are so many songs that make me feel love in its purest essence of STORGE and the passage of time. "Love Begins at Home" By Oleta Adams written by Oleta Adams, Jud Friedman, and Allan Rich. The title of this song says it all.

Every Saturday my extended family with grandparents, cousins, aunt, and uncle would sit around the kitchen table in my grandparents' house for lunch. My grandma Sarah and grandpa Louie would cook a meal of roasted peppers, baked chicken, olive oil garlic spinach, with a fresh vegetable salad. All ingredients came from their garden, barns or the basement preserve pantry. The grownups drank homemade wine, and the children sipped Warwick Club ginger ale. There were never any harsh words, only happy loving faces around that table. During my winter visits my grandpa would sit looking out his bedroom window. Sitting on a chrome and red vinyl kitchen chair, grandpa planned his spring chores while looking out on frozen ground and naked fruit trees. I would visit him in his bedroom. He would allow me to pick a treat from the top drawer of his dresser. There were Hershey bars, small bags of planters' peanuts, packs of wriggly juicy fruit gum and boxes of stogie cigars, all from the seasonally closed social club. I chose the Hershey bar with almonds. I sat on his bed in the sunlit bedroom eating my candy bar and talking about next summer working in the garden and the social club. My first job of the spring season was to shovel a large load of delivered chicken manure into a garden bin. One year I had a broken ankle in a cast, wrapped it up in plastic and performed my spring ritual. Grandpa used this natural fertilizer to spread between the vegetable plants. The tomatoes came up bright red, plump, and juicy. In the early fall the grownups would set up makeshift tables on sawhorses, take the old coal stove out from the barn, fire it up, and start to make tomato sauce preserve in big steel pots for the winter season. Preserved in Bell Jars and shelved in the cellar kitchen, I called it red gravy. Most Italian families in the neighborhood had two kitchens, one in the main body of the house and one in the basement. The basement kitchen was a prep area, where the garden fruits and vegetables were cleaned, washed, and cut. Some vegetables were pickled and preserved for winter; others used in that day's meals. The barrels of homemade wine were kept in the dryest room along with the curing salami and sausage hanging from the ceiling. Near the basement sink, chickens, rabbits and once a year a goat would be butchered for meat. One job that I did not like was plucking the feathers from a dead chicken as it was hung upside down to drain its blood in a pan on the cellar floor.

Grandpa Louie had a white RCA radio on his bedroom dresser tuned into an Italian News and Music Station. We talked and listened together as music played; I became captivated with the Italian music just like I was with Grandpa Johnny's big band sound. I can still hear these Italian songs today on streaming services. This is my recollection of the love of family, STORGE, in my life, this is also my Music lessons in foreign languages. To feel the emotion in these Italian songs it is imperative to hear the songs in their original romantic Italian language. Most streaming services and YouTube will have the original recordings. Four of my favorite Italian songs: "Al di La" By Emilio Pericoli written by Italian composer Carlo Donida and lyricist Mogol. English translation "Al di la" means you are far above me. A love song in any language can give a glimpse of a supernatural love; my heart opens wide when I relate this song to the Spirt of Love, the Holy Spirit. The writers relate the wonders and beauty of life to the object of the singer's affection. In listening I ask who is above, who is as lovely as the night sky, who makes the plants bloom and who can bring light to my heart? I cannot see it, touch it, smell it, but I cannot deny the Spirit's existence. *"Jesus answered her, " If you knew the gift of God and who it is who says to you, 'Give me a drink,' you would have asked him, and he would have given you living water."* John 4:10 (WEB). "Quando, Quando, Quando" by Tony Renis written by Tony Renis and lyrics by Alberto Testa. English translation "Quando" means when. Remember the old saying "if not now, then when?" When will I turn to God for all my needs? What is holding me back from giving God my all? Saint Augustine the Bishop of Hippo had an early life of debauchery along with an extraordinarily intense sense of right and wrong. His hunger for knowledge and desire for truth led him to look, knock, and ask for the gifts of the Holy Spirit, however, it took him a long time before he was willing to give it his complete devotion. Saint Augustine never turned back; he found the true love he longed for in Christ. "Oh, master make me chaste and celibate-but not yet." Saint Augustine (354-430) Bishop of Hippo, a Roman African, Theologian and Philosopher. Matthew 6:26-30 (WEB) *"See the birds of the sky, that they don't sow, neither do they reap, nor gather into barns, your heavenly Father feeds them. Aren't you much more value than they? Which of you, by being anxious, can add one moment to his lifespan? Why are you anxious about clothing? Consider the lilies of the field, how they grow. They don't toil, neither do they spin, yet I tell you that even Solomon in all his glory was not dressed like one of these. But If God so clothes the grass of the field, which today exist and tomorrow is thrown into the oven, won't he much more clothe you, you of little faith?"* Why do I have so little faith? If only I had faith as small as a mustard seed, Oh me of little faith. "Come Prima" by Tony Dallara written by Mario Panzeri, Sandro Taccani, Enzo Di Paola. English translation "like Before" "more than before"- God's love is endless. His love is the first and the last. All I have, all I am is because God loved me unconditionally.

There is one Italian song that I enjoyed listening with my grandfather and for me it straddles two loves STORGE and PHILIA. My best friend in high school, a second-generation Italian American like me, surprised me one day as we were driving around disgusting our teenage condition in his small three speed Fiat automobile. How much more Italian American could we have been? He related to me how as a small boy he would perform this song for his family. In Hearing him sing this song in Italian, my affection for him grew stronger. His command of the Italian lyrics impressed me. His rendition has stayed with me for well over fifty years, as has our friendship.

"Eh Cumpari" by Julius La Rosa adapted from a traditional Sicilian song composed by Julius La Rosa and Archie Bleyer. English translation: "Hey Buddy let us play and make some music." Many persons I know talk fondly of their teen friendships, it was a time of goodness and fun, a time when we looked forward to being with each other. It seems like my life has always come back to faith, music, friendship, and love. "I believe in love" by Kenny Loggins written by Alan Bergman, Marilyn Bergman, and Kenny Loggins. What else is more important to believe in?

CHAPTER SEVEN

# I Would Like to Get to Know You

**P**HILIA, another word for love found in the bible and writings by C.S. Lewis, is a word to describe a strong affection between friends and compatriots, a brotherly love, a friendship love. "There is nothing on this earth more to be prized than true friendship." Thomas Aquinas. As I write, memories of friends come to mind. I can recall their faces and their bright spirits along with the companionship we shared. "One of the most beautiful qualities of true friendship is to understand and to be understood" Seneca the younger, Stoic Philosopher (4BC-65AD). There is an old saying, "You can pick your friends but not your parents." I think I have done well with my choice of friends, or I was lucky in the fact they consider me a friend.

PHILIA, a love that goes beyond casual acquaintances, a love of shared interest and experiences, is knowing you can count on nonfamily members in time of trouble, and they can count on you. In times past this Love was considered the most important, people relied on their neighbors and friends for growth and survival. Growing up in the city, I experienced the feeling of PHILIA in the ethnic neighborhoods. It manifested itself in places of worship, corner markets, bakeries, local restaurants, fruit stands and city parks, places in which everyone knew your face, name, and family. The best explanation I heard for this type of Love: Think of an old dear friend that you grew up with or met in your life. You have not seen this person (male or female) in a long time; unexpectedly you meet, and it is like the last time you were together. You look beyond the physical and straight into the soul of that friend. You can talk about your life, ideas, and beliefs with each other. There is no judgement, it does not matter if you agree or not, the conversation is stimulating and kind, you always will remain friends. It is like the spirit inside of you has not aged. That is PHILIA Love.

My experience with PHILIA love revolves around friendships forged in elementary school, Boy Scouts, junior high, dating, high school, college, and work life. It continues today in my neighborhood; it is of the present as well as the past. I remember friends from the first grade at Saint Teresa's elementary school, on Manton Avenue, in Providence, Rhode Island, two of whom I kept contact with all my life. These friendships developed over years of walking to school, playing games, talking about music, such as the new songs of the Beatles, Beach Boys, and the British invasion, movies like the latest westerns, SYFI movies, and James Bond Films, and sports, such as the formidable friday night fights of Mohamad Ali, Providence College basketball and any Boston major sports franchise. We walked to local duck pin bowling alleys, hung around city corners under streetlights, and chipped in nickels and dimes for a large bag of french fries from a neighbor restaurant to eat on the front stoop of someone's house. We played and worked together, drove around with the guys in cars talking about the future and our place in the world, and of course, with the boys, talked about girls. These are memories I cherish. My friends made me a better person. I hope I was able to contribute to their lives. Friendships are one of the footings we build our lives upon. Through the years, my friends and I have had differing views on subjects, yet it is only fodder for conversation with no lasting damage to lifelong love and respect for one another. Philia love can happen at any age. When I meet a person who is not afraid to show their true colors, I want to get to know them and spend time in stimulating conversation. *Leviticus*

*19:34 (WEB) "The stranger who lives as a foreigner shall be to you as the native-born among you, and you shall love him as yourself; for you lived as foreigners in the land of Egypt. I, am the LORD your God."* "What draws people to be friends is that they see the same truth. They share it." C.S. Lewis.

I had a tough time with nerve pain in my face. I needed brain surgery to relieve the pressure. The outpouring of love from my faithful friends was extremely hard for me to accept without being emotionally overwhelmed and grateful for their love. I felt I did not deserve that love, until one of my friends said you have always thought of others the same way we think of you. We can always count on you to be there for us. Of course you can because I love you all. "Blessed is the servant who loves his brother as much when he is sick and useless as when he is well and be of service to him. And blessed is he who loves his brother as when he is a far off as when he is by his side, and who would say nothing behind his back he might not, in love say before his face." Francis of Assisi (1181-1226) Italian Mystic, Poet, and Catholic Friar

Music lessons of PHILIA Love. Songs that express a love of friendship. "For Good" from the broad way play Wicked-Original cast Idina Menzel and Kristin Chenoweth written by composer Stephen Schwartz and Winnie Holzman. A deep friendship that started off on a rocky path until understanding and truth bonded them in love. "Lean on me" by Bill Withers. No one is an Island; we need others for a fulfilling life. Ephesians 4:1-2 (WEB) *"I therefore, the prisoner in the Lord, beg you to walk worthily of the calling with which you were called, with all lowliness and humility, with patience, bearing with one another in love."* "He ain't heavy he's my brother" by the Hollies written by Bobby Scott and Bob Russell. When we help each other deal with life and death, we show our true colors to our friends, and they respond with love. Luke 10:33-35 (WEB) *"But a certain Samaritan, as he traveled, came where he was. When he saw him, he was moved with compassion, came to him, and bound up his wounds, pouring on oil and wine. He set him on his own animal, brought him to an inn, and took care of him. On the next day, when he departed, he took out denari, gave them to the host, and said to him. 'Take care of him. Whatever you spend beyond that, I will repay you when I return."* "You've got a Friend" by Dusty Springfield written by Carole King. l know I can call on a loyal friend, and they will be there to help me out. "That's what friends are for" by Dion Warwick, Elton John, Stevie Wonder and Gladys Knight written by Burt Bacharach and Carole Bayer Sager. "Friendship is the source of the greatest pleasures and without friends even the most agreeable pursuits become tedious."

Thomas Aquinas. (There'll be blue birds over) "The White Cliffs of Dover" by Vera Lynn written by Walter Kent and Nat Burton. One of the most popular songs of World War II. Nazi Germany was bombing Britain. The White Cliffs of Dover served as a defense barrier, the blue birds, were English fighter aircrafts, who's underside was painted sky blue. This is a song of reassurance and hope for a resilient population who fought side by side for their country and freedom for the world. The World War II cemeteries in Normandy are full of friends we never met. "Ferry Cross the Mersey" by Gerry and The Pacemakers written by Gerry Marsden. You belong to your neighborhood; you belong to your town; they will never turn you away. All our cities and towns have the potential to be places of brotherly love. "In my life" by The Beatles written by Lennon–McCartney. As long as I live, I will always remember my friends, living or dead, they taught me life lessons by just being themselves. David and Jonathan's Friendship, 1 Samuel 18: 1-4 (WEB) *"When he had finished speaking to Saul, the soul of Jonathan was knit with the soul of David, and Jonathan loved him as his own soul. Saul took him that day and wouldn't let him go home to his father's house anymore. Then Jonathan and David made a covenant because he loved him as his own soul. Jonathan stripped himself of the robe that was on him and gave it to David with his clothing, even including his sword, his bow, and his sash."* 2 Samuel 1:25-26 (WEB) *"How the mighty have fallen in the middle of the battle! Jonathan was slain on your high places. I am distressed for you, my brother Jonathan. You have been very pleasant to me. Your love to me was wonderful, surpassing the love of women."* Ruth and Naomi's friendship, **Ruth 1:16-17** (WEB) *"Ruth said, "Don't urge me to leave you, and to return from following you, for where you go, I will go; and where you stay, I will stay. Your people will be my people, and your God my God. Where you die, I will die, and there I will be buried. May the LORD do so to me, and more also, if anything but death parts you and me."* "The only way to have a friend is to be one." Ralph Waldo Emerson, writer essayist, philosopher, abolitionist, and poet. (1803 – 1882) "Heartlight" by Neil Diamond written by Neil Diamond, Carole Bayer Sager and Burt Bacharach. Let your true friendship show for all the world to see.

CHAPTER EIGHT

# Let's Get It On

**E**ROS love is romantic, sensual, and enthusiastic. In Greek Mythology EROS is the God of love and sex. He is powerful and mischievous. Eros love is a strong love and out of all loves easy to misuse. Eros is not justification for self-indulgence or promiscuity, rather it represents the craving for that one person. EROS was the original inspiration for Cupid. "Man, sins against nature when he goes against his generic nature, that is to say, his animal nature. Now it is evident that, in accord with natural order, the union of the sexes among animals is ordered towards conception, from this it follows that every sexual intercourse that cannot lead to conception is opposed to man's animal nature." Thomas Aquinas. Controversial, you can bet it is, especially in this day and age. Songs of EROS love in pop music that remind me of its purpose are, "I only want to be with you" by

Dusty Springfield written by Mike Hawker and Ivor Raymonde. I only want to be with that one person physically and spiritually. "God only knows" by the Beach Boys written by Brian Wilson and Tony Asher. What would become of me if I had to live without that person? "Unchained Melody" by the Righteous Brothers written by Alex North and Hy Zaret. Everyone hungers for the touch of true Love. "Something" by the Beatles written by George Harrison. It is that indescribable attraction that leaves us speechless. "Can't take my eyes off you" by Frankie Valli written by Bob Gaudio and Bob Crewe. Like a favorite painting or picture, we never exhaust looking at the object of our affection. "Make it with you" by Bread written by David Gates. I do not want to live without human love and affection once I have found the true meaning of love. I chose the one to help me through. "Suavecito" by Malo written by Richard Bean, Abel Zarate, and Pablo Tellez. I feel the feeling of love deep inside, softly, body and soul. "Only Love is real" by Carole King. Love is the thing that allows us to feel what is real. EROS, an integral aspect of marriage between a man and a woman, it is necessary on the path of Life. "Listen with ears of tolerance! See through the eyes of compassion! Speak with the language of Love." Rumi (1207-1273) Mystic, Poet, and Islamic Theologian. Without Eros love none of us would be here on earth. Eros love is on the journey to understanding the ultimate love, AGAPE, which gives a higher Love. Proverbs 5: 18-19 (WEB) *"Let your spring be blessed. Rejoice in the wife of your youth. A loving doe and a graceful deer, let her breast satisfy you all times. Be captivated always with her love."* Ephesians 5:31 (WEB) *"For this cause a man will leave his father and mother and will be joined to his wife. Then the two will become one flesh.* EROS is an integral part of life and marriage. It is my experience and was always my belief that PHILIA love comes first in a relationship, then marriage followed by EROS love and ends with AGAPE. EROS love is important to all other loves. Important in that it has a job to do, it is not an end.

A good example of Eros love, the craving for that one person, in literature is a short story called "The Gift of the Magi" by the short story writer O. Henry whose real name was William Sydney Porter (1862-1910). The story is of a poor young couple living in New York City at the turn of the twentieth century. Jim and Della, a married couple, live a meager existence, with little money to spare after paying the rent and buying groceries. Jim works long hours and regularly comes home at 7 pm for dinner and precious time with the love of his life Della. It is Christmas Eve and Della had been saving what little she could to buy Jim a Christmas present. She has saved $1.87 but realizes it is not enough to buy Jim a nice present.

The young couple have one precious item each, Jim has a gold pocket watch that has been passed down to him from his grandfather to his father, and now to Jim, however he rarely takes it out of his pocket because it has a warn leather strap that does not look good and cheapens the beautiful time piece. Della's prize possession is her beautiful long brown hair that comes down to her knees. Della makes a thoughtful and loving decision to sell her long hair. She visits a hair shop where an unsympathetic owner quickly offers $20.00 for her hair and cuts it off. Della has no regrets and spends the rest of the day searching for the perfect chain to adorn Jim's gold watch, meanwhile Jim sells his most precious possession the gold watch to buy Della an expensive set of Jeweled rim tortoise shell hair combs for her beautiful long brown hair. This young couple gave up their earthly possession for each other. The eternal love they shared was priceless. This example of love and sacrifice for that one special person in our life is the true meaning of EROS love.

CHAPTER NINE

# Bring Me a Higher Love

AGAPE love is the type of love a person of faith hopes to feel and personally understand, also for the unfaithful it can be a discovery of a wonder filled serendipitous experience. Unconditional, and the highest form of love, AGAPE is the love of God for men, women, and children. "We Know there is intention and purpose in the universe, because there is intention and purpose in us." George Bernard Shaw. The Holy Spirit intercedes for me; the intention is mine and the Spirit leads me in the direction of a purpose. "Agape is something of the understanding, creative, redemptive goodwill for all men. It is a love that seeks nothing in return. It is an overflowing love; it's what theologians would call the love of God working in the lives of men. And when you rise to love on this level, you begin to love men, not because they are likeable, but because God loves them." — **Martin**

**Luther King Jr. (1929-1968) American Christian minister, Civil rights Leader, Activist, and political philosopher.** The songs below fill me with a spirit of Joy and happy emotions. They are declarations of the power of love. I get a confirmation of what can benefit me and others by placing God first, listening with inquisitive ears brings understanding of God's love for humans and makes all other loves shine bright. "Kindness is the language which the deaf can hear and the blind can see." Mark Twain (1835-1910) American writer, and humorist. Songs that I enjoy listening to that make me think of God's Love for all of us are, "Just Remember I Love You" by Firefall written by Rick Roberts. Remember who Loves you unconditionally forever. "Get Together" by The Young bloods written by Chester Powers and Dino Valenti. It is so easy to smile at strangers, little children do it all the time, try it and observe the reaction you get. I sense a relationship to a happy face who recognizes a stranger's smile, we are in the spirit together. "Love is the Answer" by England Dan and John Ford Coley written by Todd Rundgren. First I needed to question what is true before realizing that love is the answer. "A Love Song" by Loggins & Messina written by Kenny Loggins and Dona Lyn George. The Spirit wants to show you the peaceful feeling of his home. AGAPE is proven through action, it is unconditional, sacrificial, and selfless. **John 3:16** (WEB) ***"For God so loved the***

*world, that He gave his only born Son, that whoever believes in him should not perish, but have eternal life." "He who doesn't love doesn't know God, for God is love. By this God's love was revealed in us, that God has sent his only born Son into the world that we might live through him. In this is love, not that we have loved God, but that he loved us, and sent his Son as the atoning sacrifice for our sins."* 1 John 4:8–10 (WEB). Love is a lifelong learning experience. Love is always with me; it exists inside my soul whether I feel it or not. Love can draw back curtains in my mind and deconstruct walls around my heart. "In the small matters trust the mind, in the large ones the heart." Sigmund Freud, (1856-1939) Austrian neurologist and founder of psychoanalysis. In my human experience of love in life, it ebbs and flows, however AGAPE stays eternally consistent. God's Love was, is, and will be forever. "I need you" by LeAnn Rimes written by Dennis Matkosky and Ty Lacy. I cannot turn back once I have felt the freedom that true love brings, everything else is an illusion and empty promises of happiness. "The Mighty clouds of Joy" by B.J. Thomas written by Buddy Bule and Robert Nix. Peace that brings Joy is in God's love. Love begins and ends with God, our Lord Jesus Christ, and The Holy Spirit. "Peace comes from within. Do not seek it without." Gautam the Lord Buddha, (563 BC-483 BC) Indian Sage, founder of Buddhism.

CHAPTER TEN

## Walk Like an Egyptian

I like to visualize my life as a pyramid with several layers, its peak like a lighthouse shining the eternal light of the Holy Trinity, the next level represents my wife and mother to my children, third level down are blocks representing my children and grandchildren, followed by blocks of close friends and community, all sitting on a foundation of the first twenty years of my life. Recently I was talking to my son on this subject, and he mentioned an interesting point. He agreed with me on the hierarchy and living with our eyes open on what is important, however he said, "Dad, look at that pyramid and realize the volume on the lower tier compared to the top. That lower tier stands for our development, education, and beliefs of the world. Our first twenty years of living have a profound influence on how our mind and character develop." Thinking about what my son said, the verse, Matthew 7:13 (WEB) came to mind. ***"Enter in by the narrow gate; for the gate is wide and the way is broad that leads to destruction, and there are many who enter by it."*** Yes, the base was wide and the volume huge, yet it was in following the broad road I found the narrow gate. It is in the foundation of life that I had the chance to make my mistakes and learn. Remember the life of Saint Augustine who went down broad roads only to find himself happy and fulfilled at the narrow gate. "There is no saint without a past, no sinner without a future." Saint Augustine

Experience is not the kindest teacher but is the one I listened to the most. I learned the proper way to hold a hot iron after burning myself a few times; only through fighting with my conscience and my conscience winning was I able to climb out of the deep holes I dug for myself by making bad choices. Not all humans need experiences to learn, luckily for the rest of us, distractions get smaller as we rise and become enlightened through our conscience by the Holy Spirit. "Experience: that most brutal of teachers. But you learn, my God, do you learn." C.S. Lewis. "You should never be ashamed to admit you have been wrong. It only proves you are wiser today than yesterday." Jonathan Swift, (1667-1745) Anglican

Priest, Irish author, and poet. My life is like being on a ten-lane highway for the first part of a journey, switching to a four-lane road, then a two lane and eventually on a driveway to my destination. I have no apprehension to travel a narrow road when the time comes to take a meaningful trip. It is more peaceful than that congested freeway, and I will surely find a higher understanding waiting for me at the end of my travels. The Holy Spirit helps us overcome. Psalm 37: 23-24 (WEB) *"A man's steps are established by the LORD. He delights in his way. Though he stumble, he shall not fall, for the LORD holds him up with his hand."*

Pop songs that lead me to think of these matters on the journey of life are like ones by Billy Joel. Billy states in His song "You're only human" (second wind), in life everyone is going to make mistakes and stumble. Reconciliation lifts us up and out of our transgressions to get us back on our feet again. Billy Joel has truisms in his songs as in "We didn't start the fire." We are only humans; there will always be fires to extinguish. "The River of Dreams" written by Billy Joel, touches on the mystery of existence, and the way of life. Did we have the truth, and did we lose it, was it taken away or is it still in our soul just buried by the choices we make? In the song "The Heart of the Matter" by Don Henley written by Don Henley, J.D. Southern and Mike Campbell, it is all about forgiveness. 2 Corinthians 5:18 (WEB) ***"But all things are of God, who reconciled us to himself through Jesus Christ, and gave to us the ministry of reconciliation."*** "You'll Never Walk Alone" by Josh Groban written by Richard Rodgers and Oscar Hammerstein II, from "Carousel" You'll Never Walk Alone. Inside all of us there is companionship and comfort. There is strength to continue the journey on the path we are born to take. "The only person you are destined to become is the person you decide to be." Ralph Waldo Emerson. There is compassion to be received and compassion to give. "Turn Around look at me" by the Vogues written by Jerry Capehart with Glen Campbell. There is someone inside of you to love and guide you, turn around and he will heal you. Ephesians 4:4-6 (WEB) ***"There is one body and one Spirit, even as you also were called in one hope of your calling, one Lord, one faith, one baptism, one God and Father of all, who is over all and through all and in us all."*** Matthew 6:33-34 (WEB) ***"But seek first God's kingdom and his righteousness; and all these things will be given to you as well. Therefore, don't be anxious for tomorrow; tomorrow will be anxious for itself. Each day's own evil is sufficient."*** "Every moment is a fresh beginning." T.S. Elliot, (1888-1965) US English poet, playwright, and critic.

I am going to start from the top of the pyramid down; At this point in my life, nothing is of a higher

Order. "Life without God is like an unsharpened pencil-it has no point." Billy Graham. Matthew 10:37-39 (WEB) *"He who loves father or mother more than me is not worthy of me; and he who loves son or daughter more than me isn't worthy of me. He who doesn't take his cross and follow after me isn't worthy of me. He who seeks his life will lose it, and he who loses his life for my sake will find it."* The Holy Spirit helps me to fully understand Jesus's words, following Christ is everything. There cannot be anyone or anything worth more. God gives us time to understand. Our Lord is a gentle spirit not a disciplinarian. Does this mean that I am not to love my wife and family? Of course not, it means that once I totally give in to the love within, a love that surpasses all earthly love and knowledge, I will do my best for those I love on earth including my neighbors and friends by knowing, loving, and serving our lord. Can it be that easy? Matthew 11: 29-30 (WEB) *"Take my yoke upon you and learn from me, for I am gentle and humble in heart; and you will find rest for your souls. For my yoke is easy, and my burden is light."*

Songs like the ones I mention below strengthen and confirm the relationship I desire with God. "Turn, Turn, Turn" by the Byrds written by Pete Seeger. This is a proclamation with lyrics from the book of Ecclesiastes. My introduction to the song was in 1965 when the Byrds had a number one hit with their interpretation. Wisdom is not hard to understand, a time to be young and experimental, and a time to grow old and wise. "Day by Day" by Robin Lamont and the Godspell Ensemble, written by **Stephen Swartz.** Broadway has brought us great songs. This song brings me comfort, Joining the two hemispheres of my brain to move me in the right direction. It confirms and reinforces my belief of purpose, "to know, love and serve God." To live in the moment is where it all happens, not in the past, and not in the future, but day by day. Psalm 118:24 (WEB) *"This is the day that the Lord has made. We will rejoice and be glad in it!"* "Kyrie" by Mr. Mister- Written by Richard Page, John Lang, and Steve George. As a young catholic boy, my Sunday Mass was spoken in Latin. Kyrie eleison and Christe eleison mean Lord have mercy, Christ have mercy. The singer is saying Lord be with me on the road I must travel and be with me in times of darkness. Have mercy on me when I do not live up to my potential as I navigate this world. Another song with a similar theme is this Grammy Award winner. "Yah Mo be there" by James Ingram and Michael McDonald written by Ingram, McDonald, Rod Temperton, and producer Quincy Jones. The story behind this song is that its original name was Yahweh (HE IS) be there. Yahweh is the original Hebrew name for God. Isaiah 42:6-7 *"I, Yahweh, have called you in righteousness. I will hold your hand. I will keep* *you, and make you a covenant for the people, as a light for the nations, to open the blind eyes, to bring the prisoners out of the dungeon and those who sit in darkness out of the prison."* Today's prisons and dungeons can be both mental as well as physical. "Do right" by Paul Davis written by Paul Davis and J. Fred Knoblock. This song from the early 1980's is a mix of a love song and gospel number. To do right is a desire by all seekers. A simple truth for anyone, if followed, can lead to a better understanding of ourselves and a fulfilled life no matter what vocation we find ourselves in. Do right for your Church, for your family, neighbors, don't cheat anyone, do right for your job, for yourself, and above all do right for the Spirit we share. The Holy Spirit will be your guiding light. "Between you and me" by DC Talk written by Toby McKeehan and Mark Heimermann. This is a Christian crossover song that hit number 29 on the billboard one hundred chart. Listening to this song is special for me. A Repentance and forgiveness lesson in music. One of the reasons I like this song is that for 10 years between 1986 and 1996, I taught CCD classes at Christ the King catholic parish in South Kingston RI. I was a teacher and a member of the religious formation committee at Christ the King catholic church. We had a special pastor who worked extremely hard on his weekly homily, making it spiritually uplifting, relevant to the times and life of his flock. Parishioners gave their Time, Talents, and Treasures to the community. Christ the King was and is a special place to worship. My CCD class or Sunday school class every week was to prepare fifth graders to receive the sacrament of penance in the Catholic Church. I was grateful to have had my own three children in class at various times during my tenure. I found forgiveness in teaching this class. It is this feeling of freedom to be forgiven, to forgive ourselves and others, that is a healing blessing from the Spirit. The Holy Spirit gives us boldness to share the good news of Christ. "Oh, Happy day" by the Edwin Hawkins Singers written by British educator Phillip Doddridge published in 1755. When he washed, he washed my sins away. This song stimulates my mind, body, and soul, making me physically moved. I feel washed. I feel Free. I also want to clap my hands and dance in his spirit who lives in me. The history of this song and how it became a huge worldwide hit is in an essay written by Bill Carpenter in 2005 and added to the National Registry. Easy to look up and a short read. It is an inspirational story; an example of how the spirit works in the most unlikely places to bring the message of Christ and the good news to the world. George Harrison, one of the Beatles once said that this song inspired his chant "My sweet Lord." Romans 8:28 (WEB) ***"We know that all things work*** *together for good for those who love God, for those who are called according to his purpose."*

A prime example of a pop music Lesson song which brings my thoughts into a place of gratitude and thanksgiving is the pop song "(Your love keeps lifting me) Higher and Higher" by Jackie Wilson written by Gary Jackson, Raynard Miner, and Carl Smith. Fans consider Jackie the father of Soul Music and you can see why, listening to this song "Higher and Higher" is like listening to Gospel music. Jackie's soul shines through as he sings his acceptance of a love that lifts him higher. I feel exhilaration when I think of God's love while listening to this song. I can listen to these exhortations all day as prayers of thanksgiving to The Holy Trinity whose Love has lifted me higher and higher. Sometimes listening to these songs in the morning, while making my bed, and before I face the challenges of the day, with the bright sun shining through my bedroom window, Hope is easy to find. There are so many other songs that lead me to the same place. It all depends on how I connect the words and music to my faith in the Holy Trinity. These songs are pleasant to hear, with thoughts of God, Jesus, and the Holy Spirit in mind, it is easy to understand God's love for his creations. There was only one perfect man and that was Jesus Christ, the rest of us were born in original sin, we are not perfect. "I believe there is no one deeper, lovelier, more sympathetic and more perfect than Jesus." Fyodor Dostoevsky (1821-1881) Russian novelist. The best we can do is ask, seek, and knock for understanding, we can be forgiven and God's Love for us AGAPE is eternal.

Back in the winter of 1958, after a fierce Nor'easter pummeled the city of Providence, it took two days for the city to dig out from over twenty-four inches of granular ice and heavy snow. The state cancelled school and late in the afternoon I asked my mom if I could go sledding. We lived on the first floor of my great grandfather's tenement house in the capitol city. The city's municipal golf course, Triggs Memorial Golf Course designed by Donald Ross and opened in May 1932, was three blocks away. It had the best slope for sledding in the area. The slope was in the practice field of the golf course just off a main road, Chalkstone Avenue. The snow that day was crusty, fresh, and high. I was the first and only person on the hill at that time. It was extremely hard to slide down the wide mound. The blades on my flexible flyer sled broke through the top crusted ice sinking into the fluffy white snow below halting any progress. I knew that on the fifth hole there was a shorter but steeper hill. I headed over across the practice field to the par3 fifth hole. I blazed a fresh path in waste deep snow, sinking into ice-crusted drifts with every step I took. Dragging my sled behind me, I arrived at the hill. I was exhausted and disappointed. The sledding conditions were the same. The trek took more effort than I realized. The sun was starting to set as I started on my way back home. I tried to walk back in my footsteps, but I had no strength left to lift my legs. I was exhausted. Leaning back in a comfortable snowdrift an urge to rest and sleep came upon me; my eyes started to shut. No sooner after giving in and closing my eyes, a tender thought dominated my mind, **"do not rest continue home."** Immediately sensing danger, I popped up and with renewed energy made my way to the main road. I had one thing on my mind, home. It was not the first time nor the last that a clear strong message came to mind. One song of my music lessons of life that makes me think of that frosty winter day is Alabama's "Angels among Us" written by Becky Hobbs and Don Goodman. There was no invisible old man in my experience but there was a gentle loving command from my Spirit that gave me the strength to overcome my sleepy body. Back then home was where I wanted to be. My thought was in that special place of comfort and safety. My family of six lived in a four room, one bathroom, first floor tenement. Our main source of heat was in the kitchen. In the winter, an old kerosene fueled steel stove made the kitchen the warmest place in the house. There was no central heat in our apartment. No source of heat in any other room. A large barrel of kerosene was in the basement of the three-decker apartment house, for heat we filled smaller containers in the cellar, lifted them up a flight of stairs to the kitchen and tipped them over to feed the flame in the stove. When we refilled and tipped the smaller containers the smell of kerosene infiltrated the whole apartment. Mother would always have a bowl of orange peels on the stove to mask the smell of the burning kerosene fuel. The smell of oranges and the warmth from that big old black stove was better than anything I could think of, especially on that cold, snow-packed winter's day. Songs like "Nightingale" by Carole King, and other pop songs connect me to places I have called home, "Homeward Bound" by Simon and Garfunkel written by Paul Simon. "Home" by Michel Bublé, written by Michel Bublé**, Alan Chang** and **Amy Foster-Gillies.** "I'm coming home" by Johnny Mathis, written by Thom Bell and Linda Creed. "Celebrate me home" by Kenny Logins, written by **Bob James and Kenny Loggins,** and "Take Me Home, Country Roads" by John Denver written by Taffy Nivert, Bill Danoff and John Denver. There are hundreds of songs that I like which express a universal yearning and a feeling for a place called Home. "Temporary home" by Carrie Underwood written by Underwood, Luke Laird and Zac Maloy talks about my belief in a permanent home. A home of Love, warmth, and comfort.

Hebrews 13:14 (WEB) *"For we don't have here an enduring city, but we seek that which is to come."*

When I listen to certain singers, it seems like I can get a glimpse of their inner soul. Listening to a young Barbara Streisand, a young Andrea Bocelli, or a young Josh Groban, the song they sing is a part of who they were at the time of recording, where they came from and what they believed. I view their voices as a gift of the Spirit as they share songs with us. The same is true with Jackie Evancho. Her talent at such an early age was angelic. Her soul shined through in her young voice. She honestly believed the words she sang. Her innocence moved me. "Somewhere" by Barbara Streisand and Jackie Evancho written by **Leonard Bernstein** and **Stephen Sondheim. This song makes me feel that there is a place for all of us.**

Our family of six lived in that first-floor tenement house until I was sixteen years old. In the winter of 1966, being a sophomore at LaSalle Academy in Providence, I struggled with my schoolwork. It was difficult to study in our small four room apartment. Mother was a seamstress and would take in alteration work at home. She would sew in the kitchen after dinner on a secondhand Singer sewing machine. Her work fabric and patterns were spread across the kitchen table. My two younger brothers watched tv in the parlor, and the baby slept quietly in our bedroom, there really was no place for me to study at home. Father worked a second job to help with the extra bills including my tuition for LaSalle. Our parents did not graduate high school and worked hard to support their family. My mother's dream was for me to be educated but I lacked the proper tools to excel. We had dinner every night as a family, and after helping to clean up, I put on my winter coat and took a mile walk up to Saint Augustine Church on Mount Pleasant Avenue in Providence. The first steps in the church were always comforting, the blast of warm air, smell of wax candles flickering, and the tranquil space made me feel closer to God. I always had a comfortable feeling and felt welcome in a sacred place. Sitting in the back pew under the balcony at seven o'clock pm, I read my school assignments in the soft mellow light. Each time I visited I noticed small scraps of paper lying on the bench. One night I read one of those scraps. It was a novena to Saint Jude, the saint of the impossible, at an anonymous person's request, it was a petition. It had special instructions to say this prayer for nine consecutive days, write out the prayer with a personal entreat, and leave it behind every night. The prayer went like this; **"May the most sacred heart of Jesus be praised, honored and glorified now and forever more, Holy Mary Mother of God pray for us sinners, Saint Jude Saint of the impossible hear my request."** (fill in request) **Thank You God for listening to**

**my prayer."** I thought I would try it; "Take a chance and you may lose. Take not a chance and you have lost already." Soren Kierkegaard (1813-1855), Danish theologian, poet, and philosopher. Thinking of my mother's circumstances I prayed that she could have a home of her own. It was a very cold February that year, at times that mile walk seemed endless, the low temperatures, snow covered sidewalks, and fierce winds blowing across Mount Pleasant's High School baseball field caused ice to build up on a scarf across my face. The walk made me feel like a character in a book that I was reading, Ivan Denisovich, the main character in a book called "One Day in the Life of Ivan Denisovich" written by Alexander Solzhenitsyn. I was committed to finishing the nine-day novena no matter what obstacles needed to be overcome. In the spring of that year my parents bought a single-family home which was three blocks from our tenement house in Providence. To our family it was like moving into a mansion. It had two bathrooms, three bedrooms, a small kitchen, a dining room, parlor, family room and a screened porch. It was a miraculous transition from our four-room apartment. Did that winter novena work? I cannot say for sure, but I know it did not hurt and increased my faith in the unknown. "You have made us for yourself, Oh Lord, and our hearts are restless until they rest in thee." Saint Augustine

CHAPTER ELEVEN

# I Saw Her Standing There

Back to my pyramid of Life, coming down from the top of my life pyramid, the next two Blocks belonged to my wife and the mother of my children. Her name is Carol. The songs I like are clear reminders of true love that transcends time, a love given not earned. To be a good steward of this gift of love involves challenging work. "Relationships are based on four principles: Respect, Understanding, Acceptance and Appreciation." William Wordsworth (1770- 1850) English romantic poet.

It was August 1964. My mom finished shopping for my back-to-school clothes. My good friend from high school commented once to me that he remembered in elementary school I was dressed sharply in a winter coat with a fur lapel. I hated that coat, but that was the blessing and curse of having a mother who could tailor any piece of discounted, irregular, or used clothing for me. The last eight years I attended a catholic gramma school. All the boys wore the same colors at Saint Teresa's school on Manton Avenue in Providence RI, white shirt, green tie, and dark trousers. This year I was starting public school, in the ninth grade at George J West Junior high in Providence, no more uniform. I now had a mini wardrobe consisting of a plaid shirt, red sweater, and tan slacks. My friend who lived on the third floor of our tenement house, invited me to go to the movies with his grandparents. This was a big treat. The featured movie at the Castle Theater on Chalkstone Avenue that late August night was "South Pacific." I dressed in my new clothes for the event. After the movie it was raining extremely hard, my friend's grandfather went to get the car. The three of us, my friend, his grandmother, and I waited under a small marquee, under that crowded marquee was an elderly woman holding hands with two young girls, waiting for their ride. I had a sudden urge to go up to the young girl on her right and introduce myself. A crazy feeling came over me, it was like that day in the snowy cold golf course. I started to play with the buttons on my new red school sweater, doing everything I could to stop myself from acting out on this strange strong urge. Luckily for me my friend's grandfather drove up just in time to protect me from my puzzling impulse and yelled hop in. Fast forward eight years to March 1st, 1972, it was my 21st birthday. I was in my senior year at Providence College. I worked at United Parcel Service (UPS) nights to pay my tuition. That night, I did not go to work. I had two wisdom teeth removed earlier in the day. I felt better around nine PM and went out to a local dance bar called the Frat House behind Rhode Island College in Providence. On that night I met my wife, Carol. "I Saw Her Standing There" by The Beatles written by John Lennon and Paul McCartney. I saw her dancing with her girlfriends and the very next dance I approached and asked her to dance with me. To make a long story short we dated for two years and were married in September 1974. We both moved from our parents' homes to a small cozy apartment by Roger Williams Park in Providence. We did not have many belongings. I noticed my new wife had a Photo Album in one of her moving boxes, as I perused the pictures, I came across a picture of her as a young girl. Immediately I realized she was that little girl I had the urge to introduce myself eight years earlier. Proverbs 18:22 (WEB) *"Whoever finds a wife finds a good thing and obtains favor of the LORD."* Proverbs 31:10-12 (WEB) *"Who can find a worthy woman? For her value is far above rubies. The heart of her husband trusts in her. He shall have no lack of gain."*

There are songs written as a love song between two people, but if I listen with the Spirit in mind, the lyrics can be interpreted as expressions of love to us from our eternal relationship with God. The Holy Spirit helps us recognize a connection to an expression of a greater love. Music Lessons in Love, for my wife Carol. "Longer" by Dan Fogelberg. The undeniable truth is clear for me. Love is a gift eternal with no beginning and no ending. This is a song that I relate to my wife from the first time I saw her under the theater marquee, and a reminder of the one who has loved us "Longer." "As (Always)" by Stevie Wonder. Like Longer by Dan Fogelberg, Stevie sings and writes of the ultimate timeless Love. In listening to the lyrics, I think of the Epistle of James and what he has to say of wisdom. I enjoy Stevie's Lyrics, amazed at the imagery written and sung. This understanding of beauty originates from deep within the lyricist. There is a spiritual lesson from the lyrics along with truth in philosophy, love, and time eternal. James 3: 17 (WEB) **"But the wisdom that is from above is first pure, then peaceful, gentle, reasonable, full of mercy, and good fruits, without partiality and without hypocrisy."** "The Wedding Song (There is Love)" by Paul Stookey. A song of union, two becoming one in a new body with a new life in marriage. Paul was a member of the famous folk group Peter, Paul, and Mary. This song brings affirmation to years of religious Lessons and talk of vocations. Human Love and marriage are not always joyful. Sometimes the issues in relationships can seem unbearable. Everyone needs help to grow and be a better person. Whenever two or more gather in his name there is love; and loving and forgiveness is the ultimate answer to discord. "Our love is here to stay" by Ella Fitzgerald written by George and Ira Gershwin. Together we can go a long way. This song has a sad beginning. George Gershwin wrote the music just before his sudden death at age 38. His brother Ira wrote the Lyrics from past conversations with George. It must have been difficult for Ira to finish this song; you can feel the love and hope he had for his brother in the Lyrics. We are not going to be around forever physically yet that unseen part of us, I believe, will be eternal in love. His Love is here to stay. Ecclesiastes 3:11-12 (WEB) *"He has made everything beautiful in its time. He has also set eternity in their hearts, yet so that man Can't find out the work that God has done from the beginning even to the end. I know there is nothing better for them than to rejoice, and to do good as long as they live."* "Through the Eyes of Love" by Mellisa Manchester written by Marvin Hamlisch and Carole Bayer Sager. There are ways to hear and see in life. Not all ways are the same. My eyes would flare up when I would get angry, and my wife would say "I'm going to get a mirror and let you see how your anger looks, and if you see what I see you will stop being angry." She was right. The opposite is true in love, if you see what you look like when you look through the eyes of love, you will not want to ever look any differently.

This last song, a favorite in this music lesson on marriage and being in love with my wife says it all for me, a lover of pop music. "Still the One" by Orleans written by John Hall and Johanna Hall. It is not easy, but she is still the one. One of my life analogies is football. My take on living is that we have four quarters to enjoy life. Now after fifty plus years of being together when problems arise in our life, I often say to my wife "honey we are in the fourth quarter, and we are ahead in the game. Let us just play good defense for the win." Her reply is "when couples grow old together the male reverts to his youth while the female continues to grow and make new discoveries." WHAT!! This song delivers my sentiment to my wife while allowing me to dance around like I 'm twenty. Crank up the volume.

CHAPTER TWELVE

# A Bridge Over Troubled Waters

This is a suitable time to state my life is not all "Sunshine, lollipops and rainbows" a Marvin Hamlisch song by Lesley Gore. "Every experience, no matter how bad it seems, holds within it a blessing of some kind. The goal is to find it." Gautam the lord Buddha. My life is not always good times, really no one's life is free from pain and sorrow. Living has brought sadness, anxiety, depression, and anger in my life. "Only through suffering, can we find ourselves." Fyodor Dostoevsky. At times negative emotions have left me with limited choices of fight or flight. Anxious days in my life have been a struggle, yet these feelings and challenges have always had a timeline of days, weeks, or months and always presented a path to resolution. Negative emotions are the other side of life's coin. I cannot be brave without experiencing fear. I cannot be a good friend without the experience of loneliness and isolation that living can bring. I cannot be thankful and grateful without the experience of doubt and neglect. My music lessons in this category deal with anger, a soul crushing emotion. Anger is an ancient force, one of the seven deadly sins. Anger is passed down from generations. Anger takes over my mind and results in unwanted thoughts and conflict with others. One of the most sinister thoughts I can have, feeling justified in anger's fury. A blinding powerhouse of negativity, anger forces love to find refuge after leaving the landscape wretched. "For every minute you are angry you lose sixty seconds of happiness." Ralph Waldo Emerson. Matthew 5: 22 (WEB) *"But I tell you that everyone who is angry with his brother without a cause will be in danger of judgment. Whoever says to his brother, Raca!' (idiot-stupid) will be in danger of the council. Whoever says, 'you fool' will be in danger of the fire of Gehenna."* "Although you may spend your life Killing, you will not exhaust all your foes, but if you quell your own anger, your real enemy will be slain." Nagarjuna (150AD-250AD?) an Indian Buddhist Monk, Philosopher and Teacher. Anger is a rabbit hole, on the way down you will pass resentment, wrath, spite, derangement, lies and sin. Matthew 18:21-23 (WEB) *"Then Peter came and said to him, Lord, how often shall my brother sin against me, and I forgive him? Until seven times?' Jesus said to him, 'I don't tell you until seven times, but until seventy times seven."*

My father-in-law had a saying for injustices. He would often say "to offer it up to God." What that meant to me was to turn the other cheek. Turn the other cheek when you are on the highway, and a reckless driver upsets you, turn the other cheek when you stand in line and someone cuts ahead of you, turn the other cheek when a person intentionally cheats you or is inconsiderate, and anytime you are treated unfairly. Turn the other cheek when you have no control of a situation that causes you mental and physical pain. This means act but do not get angry, do not use the power of anger in any way, it will only bring grief to yourself and others including the innocent: offer your pain up and lift your cross. Romans 12:19 (WEB) *"Don't seek revenge yourselves, beloved, but give place to God's wrath. For it is written, 'Vengeance belongs to me; I will repay, says the Lord."*

If I can only learn from reading, listening and meditative stillness, instead of experience, and not get caught up in the negative moment. This process is easier said than done. "Holding on to anger is like grasping a hot coal with the intent of throwing it at someone else; you are the one who gets burned." Gautama the lord Buddha. The words and music in these types of songs express the rage I have had and struggles I experienced with my anger. A personal war in my mind between good and evil, turning the other cheek or getting even. I cannot seem to let go. Anger is a destructive force, it is hungry for power and energy, draining its host into the shell of a human with no reason or thought of its own. It's a fool's game. I believe succumbing to anger did not make the man I am today, I made the mistake, knowing God made me for better. Emotions cause people to pay attention to what caused them to feel. Anger is a powerful emotion. I have felt it in my heart and knew if I did not deal with it, anger would eventually kill me. "Too much self-centered attitude, you see, brings, you see, isolation. Result: loneliness, fear, anger the extreme self-centered attitude is the source of suffering." "We often add to our pain and suffering by being overly sensitive, overreacting to minor things, and sometimes taking things too personally." 14th Dalai Lama – Born Lhamo Thondup (1935-present) Spiritual leader of Tibet- Tibetan Monk, Philosopher, and activist.

In the corporate world, anger and rage entered my life accompanied by fear, anxiety, and depression; feeling excluded and alone because of my beliefs, I felt devalued and disempowered while at the same time exceeding expectations and having success. I would lock myself away so I would not hurt the ones I love or myself. I struggled and wrestled with a demon. I also prayed, and through prayer Hope was understood, but I still was thick headed and resentful. The Holy Spirit intercedes for us. Romans 8:26 (WEB) ***"In the same way, the Spirit also helps our weakness; for we do not know how to pray as we ought. But the Spirit himself makes intercession for us with groanings which can't be uttered."*** The following songs have meaning to me in my struggles with anger. "Behind blue eyes" by the Who written by Pete Townshend. The result is always the same, I end up alone, hurt and hurting the ones I love, blaming everyone but myself. "You Always Hurt the One You Love" by The Mills Brothers written by Allan Roberts and Doris Fisher. It is the truth you will always hurt your loved ones by being angry even though your anger is not directed towards them. The progression of the battle with anger in my mind and soul leads to unwellness. "How can one be well…when one suffers Morally?" Leo Tolstoy (1828-1910) Russian writer. "unwell" by Match Box 20 written by Rob Thomas. This is not truly me; it is not the way I want to be. To say that in these times of emotional anxiety, depression, and anger, I am unwell is an understatement. It makes the people you love not want to be around you, they run to storm shelters and get as far away from the blast… Only true love can weather a charged filled storm like this.

## MUSIC LESSONS

My mother passed away at the age of forty-two. She suffered with colon and pancreatic cancer, all the doctors, all the drugs, and operations could not save her. I was mad and angry, it was so unfair I thought, the medical profession let her down and put her through much suffering. I remember riding in the black limo from the funeral parlor to her grave site. Looking out the window at the daily traffic, I wondered how people could go about their business. Did they know my mother had died? I covered up my hurt by being angry. "I sat with my anger long enough until she told me her real name was grief." C.S. Lewis. "Oh, fear not in a world like this, and thou shalt know ere long, know how sublime a thing it is to suffer and be strong." Henry Wadsworth Longfellow (1807-1882) an American poet and educator. Anger is a sin against love. Anger is a destructive force. The exact opposite of Love. 1 Corinthians 13: 1-3 (WEB) *"If I speak with the language of men and of angels, but don't have love, I have become sounding brass or a clanging cymbal. If I have the gift of prophecy and know all mysteries and all knowledge, and if I have all faith so as to remove mountains, but don't have love, I am nothing. If I give away all my goods to feed the poor, and if I give my body to be burned, but do not have love, it profits me nothing."* If I author a book of Love but have anger in my heart than I am just a hypocrite with no moral compass. "Paint it Black" by the Rolling Stones written by Mick Jagger and Keith Richards. This is a song written about the loss of human love, the death of a loved one being the cause of his misery. Anger is the absence of Love and that is like death, and the cause of my misery. The only positive thing about these scenarios is the awareness that they exist, and I am a player in the scene. The answer to these feelings is the acceptance that I am only human and have done serious wrong. Forgive me for my trespasses as I forgive those who have trespassed against me. "There is no success without hardship" Sophocles.

"Time and Love" by the 5th Dimension written by Laura Nyro. Laura Nyro's lyrics are poetic, and her song style was a brilliant blend of pop, soul, jazz, blues, and gospel. Nothing cures like time and Love. The Holy Spirit helps us overcome. Angry person, have you ever heard the expression "you are not who you think you are." I am not who I am when I am angry. Anger and love cannot live in the same place. I need help to let it go and turn the other cheek. "There are three of you. There is the person you think you are. There are the person others think you are. There is the person God knows you are and can be through Christ." Billy Graham. "Separate lives" by Phil Collins written by Stephen Bishop, is a song of building walls around your hearth to protect yourself. I am not what I think when I am in the throes of anger. I will deconstruct the walls that block Love. I am more than anger. I am more than anxiety, I am more than fear and depressed, much more. I am because he is the spirit that resides in me, the Holy Spirit. "It ain't over till it's over." Yogi Berra (1925-2015) Professional baseball catcher, coach, and former manager for the New York Yankees

The negative emotions will not last long if I am truthful with myself, recognize my faults and continue to ask for forgiveness. I can break that wall of stubbornness that keeps me a prisoner of anger. The parable of the prodigal son is my story. Luke 15:21-24 (WEB) *"The son said to him, 'Father, I have sinned against heaven and in your sight. I am no longer worthy to be called your son.' But the father said to his servants, bring out the best robe and put it on him. Put a ring on his hand and sandals on his feet. Bring the fattened calf, kill it, and let's eat and celebrate; for this, my son was dead, and is alive again. He was lost and is found. Then they began to celebrate."* It is time to come home, like the prodigal son filled with remorse asking for forgiveness and realizing any road in the direction I took was a dead end. "How sweet it is to be Loved by You" by Marvin Gaye written by Holland-Dozier-Holand. How sweet it is to be loved by our Father in Heaven unconditionally. "In the life of the body a man is sometimes sick and unless he takes medicine, he will die. Even so in the spiritual life a man is sick on account of sin, for that reason he needs medicine so that he may be restored to health; and this grace is bestowed in the Sacrament of Penance" Thomas Aquinas. "Always Tomorrow" by Gloria Estefan written by Gloria Estefan. The power is within to change and have influence, no ego involved, ask and it will be given, seek and you shall find. Ezekiel 3:20 (WEB) *"Again, when a righteous man turns from his righteousness and commits iniquity, and I lay a stumbling block before him, he will die. Because you have not given him warning, he will die in his sin, and his righteous deeds which he has done will not be remembered; but I will require his blood at your hand. Nevertheless if you warn the righteous man, that the righteous not sin, and he does not sin, he will surely live, because he took warning; and you have delivered your soul."*

CHAPTER THIRTEEN

## Wake Up Sunshine

"Don't educate your children to be rich. Educate them to be happy, so they know the value of things, not the price."

VICTOR HUGO
*French novelist, poet, and politician (1807–1882)*

Continuing to name the blocks of my life pyramid, the next rows belong to our children and grandchildren; that is what my wife and I work for, family, our true vocation in our marriage and this life together. Someone once asked me "you must be very proud of your Children?" My answer was "I am very happy that my children are who they are and used all their God given talents to be the best they can be, there is no pride in it for me, I just love Them." Proverbs 24:3-4 ***"Through wisdom a house is built; By understanding it is established; By knowledge the rooms are filled with all rare and beautiful treasure."***

The past held memorable moments of raising my three children: Memories of births, first baths, changing diapers, birthdays, vacations, educational experiences, sports, music lessons, and a thousand more events in the first quarter of their lives. I cherish all the memories of the time spent with my young family and the life my wife and I were able to provide for their wellbeing. It is a life of thankfulness and gratitude to God. "The person who has stopped being thankful has fallen asleep in Life." Robert Louis Stevenson, (1850-1894) Scottish novelist, essayist, and poet. Church, education for our children, and family time were the priorities of our marriage. Was it easy, did it come without struggle? No, but we worked at it and grew. Repentance and forgiveness are gifts of the Holy Spirit which we learned to accept with humility and without pride. If a person genuinely wants what is right, God will provide time to achieve it, no matter what age he or she asks for the truth and meaning of life. The Spirit is eternal with no constraints or physical limitations. "You can easily forgive a child that is afraid of the dark, the real tragedy of life is when men are afraid of the light" Epicurus (341BC-270BC) Ancient Greek Philosopher. Songs like "Because you loved me" by Celin Dion written by **Diane Warren bring the point home.** I lost my faith; The Holy Spirit gave it back to me. The Holy Spirit helps us to overcome our upsets and difficulties of life. Proverbs

3:5-6 (WEB) *"Trust in the LORD with all your heart, and don't lean on your own understanding. In all your ways acknowledge him, and he will make your paths straight."*

My son, Mathew, is our oldest child. One of my fondest memories of quality time spent with my son took place in 1990 when he was in the nineth grade at South Kingston High School in Rhode Island. After coming out of my struggles with anger, anxiety, and depression, I started a new job with The Andrew Jergens Company out of Cincinnati, Ohio. I started in September of 1990 as a major account sales manager in New England and Upstate New York. During my training in Cincinnati, I was staying in a Marriott courtyard. The hotel chain was having a national contest for their guests. Four all-expense paid trips to the NCAA regional men's basketball finals. I unexpectedly won the eastern finals being held at the Meadowlands in New Jersey close to New York City. An All-expense paid trip including air fare, accommodations, spending money and tickets to the big games for two. My son and I flew out of T.F. Green airport in Warwick, RI into New York's LaGuardia airport on a Friday night. We rented a car and found our hotel in the city. The next day we spent the day exploring the West Village in New York before the games. We talked of life, challenges, and forgiveness, and afterwards had fun exploring the city streets. I was impressed when my son, age 14, started to negotiate and bargain with a salesperson for a pair of ear buds in an Electronics store. He was wise and mature in his approach to dealing with a stranger. I never saw that side of my boy and wondered what else I did not know about my son. We had a great weekend bonding, exploring, and going to the basketball games. The Music lesson that runs through my mind was one I heard with my son when he was seven years old, and we were driving home from a youth soccer game. When the song came on the radio, I looked over at him and wished that time would stand still. "Just the way you are" by Billy Joel. My son Mathew has remained the same old someone that I knew. His elementary school teacher once commented to me, show me a seven-year-old boy and I will show you the man. Again, what I heard in the music and words connected me to the supernatural via love. What will it take for us to genuinely believe and trust in God? John15:9 (WEB) *"Even as the father has loved me, I also have loved you. Remain in my love."*

Our oldest daughter Lisa was going through growing pains when she was in Junior high school. The excitement and glitter of the world was calling her. She was conflicted between the events at home, family, and the world's offerings. One day when she was in the eighth grade, I invited her to take a ride down to the seashore and talk. We started off awkwardly. I really did not want to come off as preaching. We lived close to the ocean, and I drove down to Narraganset Beach on a sun filled spring day. The conversation was going nowhere so I suggested we stop at a candy store at the pier. Handing over five dollars to my daughter I sent her in on her own to pick out a sweet treat. She came back into the car with a bag of Jellybeans. As we continued our ride, we started to eat candy. These Jellybeans were quite different from the usual Easter variety, each bean had a unique flavor, as we ate a bean, we quizzed each other on what flavor we were eating. The flavors ranged from pear, cherry, cotton candy to toasted marshmallow and more unusual flavors for a Jellybean. I asked her for the name of this candy, and she replied they are called Jelly Belly beans. That small bag of candy started a conversation that opened the door to talking about what was going on in her life. Five years later I was a Director of Sales for a small Specialty food and candy broker in New England and one of the companies that we represented was the Goelitz candy company maker of the Jelly Belly brand of jellybeans. Their sales and distribution in the chain stores of New England were dismal. I recalled that day with my daughter and that little bag of jellybeans, I wanted to show my appreciation for how a small bag of Jellybeans helped me bond with my daughter. I never mentioned this story to anyone at work. Our sales organization KKM out of Lincoln RI went on to build their business in the retail outlets of New England and exceptionally large retail chains in the country, Trader Joe's, CVS, TJ Max, Marshalls, and BJ's wholesale clubs to mention a few. Our sales organization won awards and recognition from a grateful and loyal company for our hard work in gaining distribution, name recognition, and sales in major accounts in the country. It is easy to see the connections from the various paths of life that the Spirit leads us on. It is like a multi piece puzzle; only specific pieces connect to complete the picture. When my daughter Lisa was attending college, I hired her part time to merchandise Jelly Belly candy stores in her area. The story came full circle for my daughter, Jelly Belly, and me. The song that makes me think of my daughter Lisa, "I hope you Dance "by Lee Ann Womack written by Mark Sanders and Tia Sillers. I do believe with all my heart that she will give faith a fighting chance and I know for sure when given the chance Lisa will dance. Mark 10:47 (WEB) *"When he heard that it was Jesus of Nazareth, he began to shout, 'Jesus, son of David have mercy on me!"*

Julie is our youngest child. My wife's pregnancy with Julie was difficult. Julie's young life differed from her siblings. My oldest daughter always refers to Julie's life as living in the bubble. She received help from the learning curve her parents experienced with her brother and sister. It was rare that Julie got into trouble, and when she did a stern look was enough to bring tears to her young eyes. One of my favorite memories with my daughter Julie was at her wedding reception. Julie chose to have a big wedding. She was married in the month of September at The Johnathan Edwards vineyard in Stonington, Connecticut. The reception was under a large white tent on the vineyard property. She wanted the traditional father daughter dance and as I knew nothing about formal dancing, she suggested we take lessons. This was a fun and happy time as she would drive down to Rhode Island from Boston on Sunday mornings. We took dance lessons from a dear friend's daughter at a dance studio in West Warwick, RI. We chose the song "Rainbow Connection," covered by the Carpenters and written by Paul Williams and Kenneth Ascher, for our dance. The song was from a Muppet movie we watched together when she was a little girl. The dance routine had dips and twirls, and I could never remember all the steps. The big night came; the service was charming. I walked my daughter in the vineyard to take her vows. It was grape harvest season, and the fragrance of ripe grapes was amazing, bringing me back to late summer nights at the Italian American social club of my youth. When the time came for the father and daughter to dance, it was going well until the last verse of the song. Holding my daughter tight, I asked "Julie what is the next step? She replied and I quote

"Dad we will be looking for a large place to live and hope to start a family." I looked her in the eyes and said "OK! but what is the next step in the dance routine?" "Rainbow Connection" Sung by the Carpenters written by Paul Williams and Kenneth Ascher. It is a sweet sound that calls my youngest daughter Julie, one she will never ignore. If she hears the call and recognizes what is happening, it will be a peaceful surrender. By Listening to the Spirit we confirm our relationship with God. 1 Samuel 3: 8-10 ***The LORD called Samuel again the third time. He arose and went to Eli and said, "here I am you called me." Eli perceived that the LORD had called the child. Therefore Eli said to Samuel, "Go, lie down. It shall be, if he calls you, that you shall say, 'speak, LORD; for your servant hears." So Samuel went and lay down in his place. The LORD came, and stood, and called as at other times, "Samuel! Samuel!" Then Samuel said, "Speak; for your servant hears."***

I would like to write that this life of ours was planned and perfectly laid out. It was not. It developed day by day. There were times when we were happy just to get a tank of home heating fuel delivered, and times we were sad, because of illnesses and death. Family life was a constant accounting system of sticking to a budget and sacrifice, my wife always stated that she constantly was taking from Peter to pay Paul, through it all we never lost faith and love for our God and each other.

By placing God first everything else came in its time. When I think of my wife and our family, the parable of the Sower of seeds reverberates in my mind and heart. "Don't judge each day by the harvest you reap but by the seeds that you plant." Robert Louis Stevenson. This parable is special to me. I vividly remember when the seed of faith was planted in my soul. It was in December of 1955. I was in the first grade at Saint Teresa's gramma school on Manton Avenue in Providence, RI. The class had just returned from the Christmas bazar held in the parish hall, across the street from the school, in the basement of the Church. My father had given me fifty cents to spend at the church bazar. I spent my time looking for a gift for my mother. I roamed from booth to booth. I saw a pair of pearl earrings in a pretty case. A kindly old woman in attendance looked down and acknowledged me. The earrings were selling for much more than I had, innocently I asked if I could buy them. She asked what money I had, I opened my hand and showed her. She asked why I wanted the earrings, and I said I wanted to give them to my mother for Christmas. She agreed to sell them to me for what money I had. Later she told my teacher what had transpired, when my first grade returned to homeroom, the sister (nun) told the class the story saying that children spent their money on candy and drink, but I thought of someone else to spend my money on. I did not think of it in those terms, and she applauded me for giving thought to my mother. Then she pointed up to the crucifix hanging on the wall and told the class about Jesus who did not think of himself and gave up his life so we can be free to enter heaven. The seed of faith was sown in my heart in that moment when I looked up at the crucifix hanging on the wall. The Parable of the Sower, Luke 8:11-15 (WEB) *"Now the parable is this: The seed is the word of God. Those along the road are those who hear; then the devil comes and takes away the word from their heart, that they may not believe and be saved. Those on the rock are they who, when they hear, receive the word with joy; but these have no root. They believe for a while, then fall away in time of temptation. What fell among the thorns, these are those who have heard, and as they go on their way are choked with cares, riches, and pleasures of life; and they bring no fruit to maturity. Those in the good ground, these are those who with an honest and good heart, having heard the word, hold it tightly, and produce fruit with perseverance."* For a long time, I thought I fell into the third category, the worries of raising a family, the clash of what I believed in and making a living, the deceitfulness of wealth, and the cowardness of not showing my true colors, heightened my anger and grief with life. I questioned right and wrong. I worked hard physically and spiritually to find meaning in the pursuit of happiness, it was always two steps forward, one step back. It took a long time to become a good weeder of thorns. All gardeners and landscapers know that weeding is endless. No resolute professional, artist, care giver, father, or mother is ever satisfied with their work. I constantly look for ways to improve my purpose in living, one that will benefit my family and neighbors. The song "Coming Out of the Dark" sung by Gloria Estefan, written by Gloria and Emilio Estefan Jr. with Jon Secada, expresses the emotion of the struggle and the light at the end of the tunnel. My wife and I know the true love that saved us and our family.

CHAPTER FOURTEEN

## *The Unicorns*

> "The greatest legacy one can pass on to one's children and grandchildren is not money or other material things accumulated in one's life but rather a legacy of character and faith."
> BILLY GRAHAM

My wife and I have nine grandchildren, they range in age from 20 to 7 years old. It is quality time when we all get together, seven girls and two boys. I enjoy my time getting to know them personally. I play with them, talk to each child individually about their interests and activities, encourage their individual characteristics making each grandchild feel loved and appreciated. I pray for their health and wellbeing. The grandkids call me Poppy. Grandchildren fill a large block on my pyramid. They are our family's future. I see innocence and curiosity in the eyes of my young grandchildren, and the growth with principles in the young adults. Listening twice as much as talking, my wife and I are a good example to our grandchildren of STORGE, the familial love and a long-lasting relationship. In being there for them, they are open and share the good and not so good times in their young lives. Our two daughters live in the suburbs of Boston, one in Arlington, MA with her three girls, and one in Hingham, MA with her three girls, all within a two-hour drive from our home. Our son lives with my two grandsons and oldest granddaughter in Palmyra, Virginia. Palmyra is just outside of Charlottsville, Va. and close to Thomas Jefferson's Monticello. We try to see the Virginia family once per quarter, sometimes flying into the area and sometimes making a nine-hour drive. Most summers we can count on having everyone to our house for extended stays, swimming in the lake and ocean, sailing, bike riding, hiking, paddle boarding, sitting around the fire pit and of course eating fresh seafood cooked at home. "If I had a Hammer" by Peter, Paul and Mary written by Pete Seeger. I would gladly hammer out the best life I can for them. Matthew 19:14 (WEB) *"But Jesus said, "Allow the little children, and don't forbid them to come to me; for the Kingdom of Heaven belongs to ones like these."* Proverbs 17:6 (WEB) *"Children's children are the crown of old men; the glory of children is their parents."*

Each time I meet with my grandchildren, the little ones ask for a story. Stories, for me, are a time to entertain and spark imagination. "A child is not a vase to be filled, but a fire to be lit." Francois Rabelais (1494-1553) French writer, Catholic priest, and Physician. There are two stories they requested often. One from my childhood and one from five years ago. They know the words by heart and as I speak, they act out the characters in the story, usually using the living room couch as their stage. The first story is from my younger years in my grandfather's garden. It is about a chicken named Peepeenella. It was springtime and grandpa Luigi took my brother Stevie, my cousins Geraldine, and Elain to a grain and seed store to buy baby chicks for the hen house. The chicks just came out of the incubator warm and fluffy. My grandpa bought twenty chicks for the season. He allowed each of us one to pick. He helped us to name each of our birds. My chicken's name, Peep- peep Nella, meaning a priceless chirping chick, but I called her Peepeenella. Every Saturday, spring through fall of that year, my father would drive to the farm. I was always the first out of the car running as fast as I could to the hen house, opening a large chicken wire fence, grabbing a handful of feed, and yelling here chickee, chickees. Out of the hen's house they came like a wave of brown and white feathers. Peepeenella led the way. Grandpa always looked on the happenings, standing silently by the chicken wire gate. Grandma came out later, and together we gathered the eggs, placing them gently in her apron. It was a fun time, playing with our cousins, running in and out of the various barns on the property, walking the well-worn paths of the gardens, and picking the fruits of the seasons. Spring ran into summer and summer slid into fall; my routine was always the same each Saturday. When the leaves started to fall off the trees the action in the hen house was calmer, but I did not care because Peepeenella was always there to hear my call. It was a cold Saturday before Thanksgiving. One of those grey overcast days of November in Rhode Island. I ran out of the car as usual and when I got to the hen house the chicken wire gate was wide open. The bag of chicken feed was gone and there were no chickens in the barn. Grandpa was standing by the fence, I asked "Grandpa where are all the Chickens?" He answered, in broken English, that all the chickens ran away, they ran down to the lake he said. He looked at me and said he was sorry; someone left the gate open the night before. My brother and I went into the house and played with our cousins, never again talking about the chickens. At lunch time, as usual we had roasted peppers, salad, vegetables, and baked chicken. I always grabbed a leg and ate it by hand. As I brought that leg up to my mouth a sick feeling came over me. I suddenly realized what raising chickens was all about and the possibility I may be eating my pet chicken Peepeenella. At the end of the story, the girl's eyes are wide open, looking at me for a reaction. It is at that point I would sing a made-up short aria for my chicken. In a deep voice I sang, "Peepeenella-Peepeenella where did you go. Peepeenella-Peepeenella where did you go, where would you go? Where would you go?" In unison the girls would giggle and shout out with loud voices "IN YOUR BELLY POPPY, IN YOUR BELLY." We all laughed together. Songs like "Bless the beast and the children" by the Carpenters written by **Barry DeVorzon and Perry Botkin Jr.**, and others make me wish those times could last forever, I wish I could be their protector and guide on the path of life forever, but someday as it was for me and my grandfather it will be for them. So be it. "All Things Must Pass" by George Harrison. Who am I without his Love? The song "Forever Young" by Joan Baez written by Bob Dylan, is a sentiment I give to my children and grandchildren. Numbers 6:24-26 (WEB) *"The LORD bless you and keep you. The LORD make his face to shine on you, and be gracious to you. The LORD lift up his face toward you, and give you peace."*

The second story took place five years ago. My wife and I live in a small community in Charlestown, RI. It is an association of forty homes on a 600-acre pond, founded in the early fifties as a summer compound, now slowly being transformed to yearlong living residents. Each summer our home near ocean beaches, and on a freshwater lake, is a destination for our family. Originally it was a three-bedroom cape cod style home we built for our retirement, however as our family grew, we made additions accommodating our growing clan. Our home keeps us busy and engaged in our community. In the summer, I like to decorate our back porch with eclectic signs, interesting wall hangings that rouse the children's imagination and stir up a conversation. My grandfather had a small farm and garden filled with wonder and discovery. I want to pay it forward. I like going to yard sales and thrift shops to find unique pieces to display. I always pick out one or two new decorations for the season and discard those that have been around for a while. One day I came across two small, matted photographs at a yard sale for two dollars each. They needed small frames. I went to the local dollar store to buy what I needed. This is where the story begins. I walked into the dollar store looking for small plastic picture frames; bending down to see if they fit the pictures, I heard an enthusiastic young boy say "mom, mom, mom, are we going to the party", his mother answered lovingly "yes, but first we need to buy a birthday card and wrapping paper." I did not see them; I was bending down looking at the frames and only heard the conversation. The boy and his mom walked on by behind me. Satisfied with my choice of frames, I headed to the snack isle for a treat. I bought a box of caramel popcorn. I went to the check out and in front of me was a mom with a young boy sitting in a shopping carriage and his brother, who looked to be five years old, standing beside the carriage. When I heard the older boy talk, I recognized his voice from the birthday conversation. They were both cute kids, the boy standing beside the carriage had a full thick head of dark curly brown hair. Their mom was unloading her purchases on the checkout belt. The little boy sitting in the carriage looked at me and the box of popcorn and said, "you bought food we didn't buy any food." His big brother said, "you bought popcorn," I said wow, you are a good reader and told him that I bought this for my dessert. The older boy said that sometimes his mom gives them desserts after dinner, I said I like dessert after dinner. He said, "you know what?" I said, "What." He said that sometimes his mom makes salad for dinner, I said that sounds healthy. He said, "you know what?" I said "what." He said, "sometimes my mom puts olives in the salad." I said it sounds delicious. He said, "you know what?" I said "what." He said, in a loud voice, "I HATE OLIVES," not even, (showing with his little fingers), olives this big (tiny). It was summer. He took his shirt and lifted it over his face and spun around. His mother looked at me and rolled her eyes, took his shirt off his head, and pushed the carriage out the door. The girls know this story word for word and when I come to the part of the "all you know what's," they are jumping on the couch yelling "I HATE OLIVES," and covering their heads with their shirts or dresses laughing and screaming. They found this story very relatable. Who knew? The story lifts their spirits and makes them happy and every time I think of their reaction it also lifts my spirit and brings a smile to my face. Each time they visit, they ask if we can go to the dollar store hoping to see children who have good stories to tell. "The soul is healed by being with children." Fyodor Dostoevsky

There are songs from my childhood that I remember lifting my spirit. Thinking of them is like thinking of an early gramma school lesson, and I recount to my grandchildren on how I listened to these songs on a car radio, sitting in the back seat of my father's De Soto automobile, breathing in secondhand smoke from a lucky Strike cigarette. I tell them how I heard a message and felt a strong connection to an unknown that I could not explain in words.

It is said that the following songs were born in the fields of the American South. It is also believed that these songs were written by slaves whose names we will never know. A folklorist happened upon this song in late 1920's North Carolina. His name was Frank Warner. A young boy in England by the name of Laurie London, a 13-year-old, had an enormous number one hit between 1957 and 1958 with his up-tempo version of this spiritual song. This song was so big that most kids under ten living in England and the U.S. could sing it word for word. We heard it all over, on car radios, sang it at the playgrounds, in cub scout camps, and around the campfires during the late fifties and early sixties. The song is "He's got the whole world in his hands" by Laurie London. Romans 10:14-15 (WEB) *"How then will they call on him in whom they have not believed? How will they believe in him whom they have not heard? How will they hear without a preacher? And how will they preach unless they are sent? As it is written: "How beautiful are the feet of those who preach the Good News of peace, who bring glad tidings of good things!"*

My youngest grandson did not let a birthday card be given to me, without a verse from the bible for Poppy. He told his father that before signing the card he needed to find an appropriate verse from the bible to write down for Poppy's birthday card. My granddaughters, while sitting on the couch during Christmas looking at tv, wanted to take a break from all the worldly Christmas shows and turn on the story of the nativity and birth of Christ. There was no prompting on my part, rather true curiosity, an inner pulling to wisdom that goes beyond knowledge. My youngest grandchild overhearing a conversation on negative thinking, exclaimed that the way she deals with bad thoughts is to yell at them and tell them to leave her alone, this is when she was six years old.

Psalm 8:2 (WEB) *"From the lips of babes and infants you have established strength, because of your adversaries, that you might silence the enemy and the avenger."*

Another song with a message of hope, salvation, and freedom that I listened to as a kid, is by the Highwaymen. It was sung by former slaves living on Saint Helena Island off the coast of South Carolina. The song is based on a traditional African American Spiritual. Freed men, women, and children sang as their former owners abandoned the island before the Union Navy arrived during the Civil War. Again, I intuitively felt a connection with something greater than myself when I heard or sang this song in groups of happy campers. "Michael row the boat ashore" by the High waymen. The Writer of the musical notations was Charles Pickard in 1860's and adapted in the mid 1950's by Boston American Folk singer Tony Saletan. Hallelujah, the word means Praise the Lord.

Songs from every generation have meaning to their listeners. *"Sing a song" by Earth, Wind & Fire written by Al McKay and Maurice White. Life is more than working for a living. Live, love, dance and sing, magic will happen if you give it a chance. Psalm 100: 1-2 (WEB)* **"Shout for joy to the LORD, all you land! Serve the LORD with gladness. Come before his presence with** *singing."* Colossians 3:16: (WEB) *"Let the word of Christ dwell in you richly; in all wisdom teaching and admonishing one another, with psalms, hymns, and spiritual songs, singing with grace in your heart to the lord." James 5:13 (WEB) "Is anyone among you suffering? Let him pray. Is any cheerful? Let him sing praise."* "Sing" by the carpenters written by Joe Raposo. A music lesson to cheer us up can appear anywhere, especially on Sesame Street. Any song of love, truth or beauty that makes you think of God, Jesus and the Holy Spirit and fills your heart with peace and joy is a song of praise.

CHAPTER FIFTEEN

# My First, My Last, My Everything

The Holy Spirit confirms our relationship with God. 1 Corinthians 13: 11 (WEB) *"When I was a child, I spoke as a child, I felt as a child, I thought as a child. Now that I have become a man, I have put away childish things."* "Reflections of my life"- by Marmalade written by Ford/McAleese and Junior Campbell. To move forward in life is to change; as much as we would like, we cannot go back. There exists a place to comfort all your sorrows here and now. Seek and you will find.

*In the year 1954 my mother, father, and baby brother Stephen lived in a tiny apartment on the third floor of a house on Manton Avenue in Providence, RI. Our house was next to the Woonasquatucket river. The back yard was swampy and often flooded in winter. In early spring after a long time indoors, I was able to go out on dry land in the yard. I was three years old. The circumstances found me alone and outside in a harness tied to a large tree. Innocently I discovered a clip that was attached to the restrictive rope. I remember unclipping myself from the rope; with unease, I clipped myself back to the rope, on and off, finally off. I was drawn to the edge of the fast-flowing spring season river. I found a cup on the ground and tried to fill it with water. My one-piece blue snow suit was too bulky for me to bend; I bent over and fell in the river. I was faced down and floating. My eyes were wide open and in wonder of the unique environment, I did not experience any fear. I saw a glowing golden rock glistening in the water; I reached out to touch it. The next memory I have is walking with someone behind me. I was soaking wet and crying. Looking at the house, my mother was screaming out of the third-floor window where she hung our laundry. That night in my small bed, with my mother and father sitting close, my father taught me this prayer.* **"Now I lay me down to sleep. I pray to the Lord my soul to Keep. If I should die before I wake, I pray to God my soul to take."** *I remember my mother telling my father that this was not a Catholic prayer. Recalling this incident in my life, I think of the person who was looking out for me and pulled me out just before I could touch that glowing golden rock. I cannot recall his or her face, yet that person saved my young life. I also think of what or where I would be if I had been able to touch that glowing rock. I must* *also mention that I was named after my father's younger brother who drowned three years earlier, before I was born.* This was the first major memory of my life, and my father's prayer is how my spiritual Journey began. *Romans 8: 38-39 (WEB)* ***"For I am persuaded that neither death, nor life, nor angels, nor principalities, nor things present, nor things to come, nor powers, nor height, nor depth, nor any other created thing will be able to separate us from God's love which is in Christ Jesus our Lord."***

"When the ego dies the soul awakes." Mahatma Gandi. In Prayer I now try to make it less of me and more of Thee. Psalm 139:14 (WEB) ***"I will give thanks to you, for I am fearfully and wonderfully made. Your works are wonderful. My soul knows that very well."*** "One Kind of Love" by Brian Wilson written by Brian Wilson and Scott Bennett. Hopefully, you the reader have listened to the music in this book and felt the healing love that the Holy Spirt can deliver. There are no limitations in unconditional Love, and the ultimate unconditional Love is from God, **AGAPE.**

> "In three words I can sum up everything I've learned a about life: It goes on."
> ROBERT FROST
> *(1874-1963) American Poet*

# Acknowledgements

I want to thank the World English Bible, (WEB) for the use of Holy Bible verses in this book, the WEB online study was indispensable, and generous by being in the public domain.

Thank you to BGEA for allowing General Permission and following printed guidelines on the use of Billy Graham Quotes. 2016 BGEA Association. Used with permission. All rights reserved.

All other quotes used by public domain or fair use guidelines.

www.ingramcontent.com/pod-product-compliance
Lightning Source LLC
Chambersburg PA
CBHW070853050426
42453CB00012B/2170